IN FILE MANAGER

Key Sequence	Effect
Directory tree only:	
+	Expand one level
*	Expand branch
Ctrl-*	Expand all
–	Collapse branch
Directory window only:	
Shift-↑ *or* Shift-↓	Extended selection
Ctrl-/	Select all

IN PRINT MANAGER

Key Sequence	Effect
Alt-P	Pause processing print queue
Alt-R	Resume processing print queue
Alt-D	Delete print job

The SYBEX Instant Reference Series

Instant References are available on these topics:

AutoCAD Release 11

dBASE

dBASE III PLUS Programming

dBASE IV Programming

dBASE IV 1.1

DESQview

DOS

DOS 5

Harvard Graphics 3

Harvard Graphics for Windows

Lotus 1-2-3 Release 2.3

Lotus 1-2-3 for Windows

Macintosh Software

Microsoft Word for the Macintosh

Microsoft Word for the PC

Norton Desktop for Windows

Norton Utilities 6

PageMaker 4.0 for the Macintosh

Paradox 3.5

PC Tools 7.1

Quattro Pro 3

Windows 3.0

Word for Windows, Version 2.0

WordPerfect 5

WordPerfect 5.1

WordPerfect 5.1 for Windows

Computer users are not all alike.
Neither are SYBEX books.

We know our customers have a variety of needs. They've told us so. And because we've listened, we've developed several distinct types of books to meet the needs of each of our customers. What are you looking for in computer help?

If you're looking for the basics, try the **ABC's** series. For a more visual approach, select full-color **Teach Yourself** books.

Learn Fast! books are two books in one: a fast-paced tutorial, followed by a command reference.

Mastering and **Understanding** titles offer you a step-by-step introduction, plus an in-depth examination of intermediate-level features, to use as you progress.

Our **Up & Running** series is designed for computer-literate consumers who want a no-nonsense overview of new programs. Just 20 basic lessons, and you're on your way.

SYBEX **Encyclopedias**, **Desktop References**, and **A to Z** books provide a *comprehensive reference* and explanation of all of the commands, features, and functions of the subject software.

Sometimes a subject requires a special treatment that our standard series don't provide. So you'll find we have titles like **Advanced Techniques, Handbooks, Tips & Tricks,** and others that are specifically tailored to satisfy a unique need.

You'll find SYBEX publishes a variety of books on every popular software package. Looking for computer help? Help Yourself to SYBEX.

For a complete catalog of our publications:

SYBEX Inc.
2021 Challenger Drive, Alameda, CA 94501
Tel: (510) 523-8233/(800) 227-2346 Telex: 336311
Fax: (510) 523-2373

SYBEX is committed to using natural resources wisely to preserve and improve our environment. This is why we have been printing the text of books like this one on recycled paper since 1982.

This year our use of recycled paper will result in the saving of more than 15,300 trees. We will lower air pollution effluents by 54,000 pounds, save 6,300,000 gallons of water, and reduce landfill by 2,700 cubic yards.

In choosing a SYBEX book you are not only making a choice for the best in skills and information, you are also choosing to enhance the quality of life for all of us.

Windows™ 3.1 Instant Reference

Second Edition

Marshall L. Moseley

SYBEX

San Francisco • Paris • Düsseldorf • Soest

Acquisitions Editor: Dianne King
Developmental Editor: James A. Compton
Copy Editors: Janna Hecker Clark, Savitha Varadan
Technical Editors: Sheila S. Dienes, Charlie Russel
Word Processors: Ann Dunn, Susan Trybull
Series Designer: Ingrid Owen
Production Artist: Alissa Feinberg
Technical Art: Cuong Le
Screen Graphics: Aldo Bermudez
Desktop Publishing Specialist: Stephanie Hollier
Proofreader/Production Assistant: Arno Harris
Indexer: Ted Laux
Cover Designer: Archer Design

To my wife, Pam Dillehay, whose love I value above all else.

Acknowledgments

I'd like to thank the editorial staff at SYBEX, especially Dianne King, Savitha Varadan, Janna Clark, and Jim Compton, for their good work and thorough professionalism. My heartfelt gratitude also goes to Doug Kass, Diane Ingalls, and Terian Tyre, three editors who taught me much and who share my love affair with the written word.

Table of Contents

Part Two

Alphabetical Guide To Features And Operations

Appendix

Object Linking And Embedding

Index

Introduction

The idea behind this book is simple. When you are stymied by a command in Windows 3.1 or 3.0 that does not work as you intended, or when you want a quick refresher on a certain procedure, you need a single source of information that can help you quickly solve the problem so you can get on with your work. This book is intended to do just that.

Windows 3.1 Instant Reference will quickly give you the information necessary to get the most from Windows' multitude of features. It will supply instructions for Windows' basic commands and its most sophisticated functions.

Because we expect you to consult this book as a reference for solving day-to-day problems, we have assumed that your copy of the program is already installed. Also, because Windows can be customized in many ways to suit individual preferences, we have not attempted to describe customization in detail here. For complete information on installation, customization features, and advanced topics (such as Media Player and Sound), see *Mastering Windows 3.1*, also from SYBEX.

HOW THIS BOOK IS ORGANIZED

This book is divided into two parts. Part I describes what Windows is and tells you how to use the Windows interface. It also contains a short description of each program provided with Windows 3.1. Here, you'll find information on the utility programs that are used on a day-to-day basis, such as the Program Manager and the Control Panel, as well as the accessory applications, sometimes called "mini-apps" or "applets."

Part II consists of an alphabetical listing of the operations you will probably want to perform with Windows and concise instructions for executing them. Entries cover such procedures as copying a file, associating a file with a program, and even using the provided telecommunications and painting programs.

Where appropriate, entries also include:

- **Notes**   This section contains information that you should know to fully understand the reference entry. This information can take many forms: for example, warnings of how the procedure under discussion could affect other executing programs, or a description of how the procedure could enhance or degrade Windows' performance.

- **See Also**   This section contains cross-references to headings in this book that are related to the current procedure.

Also included in this book is an appendix that discusses the object linking and embedding (OLE) technology new in Windows 3.1.

TYPOGRAPHICAL AND INSTRUCTIONAL CONVENTIONS

Each entry in this book is designed to provide you with a clear, concise explanation of a particular Windows procedure or function. To that end, information is presented here in a particular manner.

- Words or terms that require special emphasis are italicized. Emphasized words can be special Windows terms, such as *scroll bar* or *Control Panel*. Words and terms are usually emphasized only once, when they are defined, and are printed normally thereafter.

- Command names, menu items, and dialog box names are printed with initial capital letters. Some examples are: the Program Manager, the File menu, and the Save As command.

- The names of keys are printed exactly as they appear on a standard IBM keyboard—for example, PgDn and NumLock. Directory names and file names are printed in uppercase letters.

- Because Windows is designed to take advantage of the mouse, mouse instructions are given precedence. Keyboard instructions are included, however, for those who prefer to work with a keyboard.

Part I
Overview of Windows 3.1

As a quick refresher for infrequent Windows users, the following pages present an overview of the operating environment—the elements of the interface, how to use the mouse and keyboard in working with Windows, and a brief summary of the Windows programs. Most readers who use Windows regularly are probably familiar with this information already and may begin looking up topics of interest in Part II right away. As noted in the Introduction, anyone using Windows for the first time should begin with a tutorial before consulting this book.

THE WINDOWS INTERFACE

Windows is a program that provides a graphic user interface (GUI) for IBM and IBM-compatible personal computers. When running Windows, the computer user interacts with the computer visually. Rather than type commands, the user moves a small arrow, called a pointer, around the screen and selects commands. Programs appear on-screen in rectangular areas called windows. Each window can be sized and moved around the screen. Multiple programs can appear on-screen at the same time, and they can operate simultaneously.

Windows runs two types of programs: standard DOS applications and Windows-specific applications. A standard DOS application is any DOS program that is not written specifically for the Windows environment. Using Windows, you can run such popular programs as dBASE and pre-Windows versions of WordPerfect and Lotus 1-2-3. Standard DOS applications can use the full display screen, or run in a window. A Windows-specific application is one written explicitly for the Windows environment. Once run, it appears as a window. It can be sized and moved around the screen. It can also be placed in the background, or allowed to take up the entire screen.

Windows' File Manager displays programs, files, and disks as icons, much like the Macintosh from Apple Computer, Inc. (An icon is a picture that represents a resource within the computing system. A memo might be represented on-screen by a picture of a piece of paper, while a printer might be represented by a picture of a printer.)

When Windows first runs, you are presented with a primary window called the Program Manager. The Program Manager contains a set of icons, called *group icons,* each of which represents a collection of programs. One of these groups, the Main group, is opened to a *group window,* revealing still more icons. These are *program icons.* These icons represent the Windows system programs, a subset of the programs you can run from within Windows.

Windows takes advantage of the 80386 and 80486 microprocessors used in today's most powerful microcomputers. (It also uses the 80286 microprocessor efficiently.) Windows uses the protected mode of those systems. In protected mode, memory is reserved for each program and no other programs may use that memory—it is protected. Windows also accesses up to 16MB of memory. See "Windows Operating Modes."

With version 3.1, Windows now employs an advanced technology called object linking and embedding (OLE). Using OLE, you can paste, or embed, information from one Windows program into another. For example, you can paste a graphic generated by Windows Paintbrush into a Windows Write document. Then, from within the Write document, you can double-click on that graphic to invoke Paintbrush and edit the graphic. OLE allows Windows programs to work together very easily. For more information, see the Appendix, "Object Linking and Embedding."

Windows is "network aware." This means that if a personal computer running Windows is connected to a local area network (LAN), Windows will see the connection and provide access to that network and its resources. Once set up for a particular network, Windows will not "see" other networks.

Windows is a boon for users of MS-DOS personal computers. They no longer need to understand the complex syntax of MS-DOS commands. Windows provides a standard, usable, powerful interface for all programs under MS-DOS.

WINDOWS OPERATING MODES

Windows operates differently on different systems. It has two operating modes, one for computers based on the 80286 microprocessor (AT-class machines), and one for computers based on the 80386 microprocessor. When Windows runs, it detects what kind of computer you have and executes in a mode appropriate to your type of system. (Windows 3.0 has an operating mode called Real mode that supports 8088 or 8086 microprocessors. Real mode has been eliminated from Windows 3.1.)

The two modes in which Windows 3.1 operates are described below.

- In *Standard mode,* Windows requires at least 1MB of memory and an 80286, 80386, or 80486 microprocessor. Windows can access up to 16MB of physical memory in

Standard mode, and can switch between multiple DOS applications. Those applications have to operate using the full screen; they cannot appear in windows. In Standard mode, multiple DOS applications do not multitask, but Windows applications do.

- *386 Enhanced mode* requires an 80386 or 80486 microprocessor and at least 2MB of memory. In 386 Enhanced mode, Windows takes advantage of the advanced features of the 80386 and 80486 microprocessors by using a portion of the hard disk as if it were memory. (Hard disk space used as memory is called *virtual memory*.) This gives Windows access to more memory than is physically present. Windows also uses these microprocessors' virtual 8086 mode to multitask DOS applications. Under Windows, DOS applications can also appear in multiple windows on screen.

Although Windows automatically detects the type of system you have and uses the requisite operating mode, you may want Windows to operate in some other mode. For example, the benefits of 386 Enhanced mode are its ability to multitask DOS applications and its use of virtual memory, but Standard mode actually makes slightly more efficient use of memory in Windows. If you have an 80386-based system with little memory, little hard-disk space, and you aren't going to run DOS applications, you may want to run in Windows Standard mode.

You can make Windows run in any mode you choose using *command line parameters.* A parameter is a series of characters placed after a command that causes the command to execute in a specific manner. To run Windows in the mode of your choice:

- From the DOS prompt, type **WIN/S** to run in Standard mode or **WIN/3** to run in 386 Enhanced mode, then press ↵.

TYPES OF WINDOWS AND ICONS

Before you can use Windows effectively, you must first understand how windows are displayed and what types of windows and icons Windows uses. All windows are displayed on the *Windows desktop,* which is the entire screen of your video display. It is useful to think of the Windows desktop as the surface of a desk on which you can lay out your work. You can change the color or pattern of the Windows desktop using the Control Panel program. See "Changing Windows' Color Scheme" and "Changing the Desktop Pattern" in Part II.

There are two types of windows, as explained below:

- *Application windows* contain executing Windows programs, and are sized, moved, opened, and closed on the desktop.
- *Document windows* are generated by an application window. A document window cannot be sized or moved outside the confines of its parent application window. Document windows are manipulated in the same way as ordinary windows, except they use slightly different key commands.

Finally, there are three types of icons:

- *Application icons* are minimized application windows. A minimized program is one that is still running, but has been reduced to an icon. This icon appears at the bottom of the Windows desktop.
- *Document icons* are minimized document windows. When maximized, they appear within an application window's workspace.
- *Program icons* appear only within the Program Manager. They will start applications and, optionally, load their associated documents.

See Figure I.1 for examples of all three types of icons.

PARTS OF A WINDOW

Most windows have certain components in common. Because of these similarities, nearly all windows can be operated in the same manner. The shared features are:

- the title bar
- the minimize, maximize, and restore buttons

6 The Windows Interface

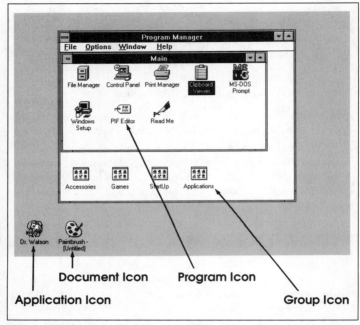

Figure I.1: A Windows screen with all icon types displayed

- the sizing borders
- the menu bar and pull-down menus
- the scroll bars

Each of these components is explained below and shown in Figure I.2.

- The *title bar* is the colored bar at the top of every window. It contains the name, or title, of the current window. You can use the title bar to move a window around on the Windows desktop. See "Moving Windows and Icons" in Part II.

- The *minimize, maximize,* and *restore buttons* are small arrows in the upper-right corner of every window. By clicking on the minimize button, you can reduce the current

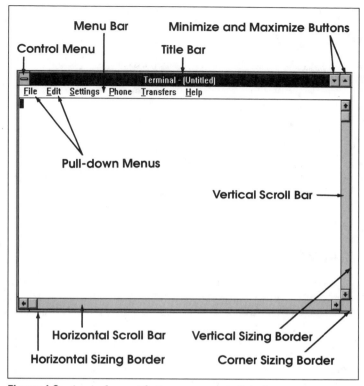

Figure I.2: A window with its components listed

window to an application icon, which will appear at the bottom of the screen; by clicking on the maximize button, you can expand the current window to take up the entire desktop. Once a window has been maximized, a new type of button called a restore button appears in place of the maximize button. Clicking on the restore button returns the window to the state it was in before it was maximized.

• The *sizing borders* are thin frames that appear around most windows and are used for sizing the window. Simply place the pointer (which becomes a two-headed arrow) over the border, click and hold, then drag the border; the window will change size. Vertical borders can be used only to change a window's width; horizontal borders can be used only to change its height. Corner borders can be used to change the width and height at the same time.

- Located directly under the title bar, the *menu bar* holds names of the pull-down menus available in the currently active window. Click on a menu name, and a *pull-down menu* will appear—it will be "pulled down."

- When there is too much data available to display in a single window, Windows will provide a *scroll bar* that will help you move through the data easily. Vertical scroll bars let you move down or up through a document, while horizontal scroll bars let you move to the right or left to display a very wide document.

DIALOG BOXES

When using Windows, you will often have to adjust settings within a program. You may have to set the default margins in a word processing document, for example, or choose a graph type from within a spreadsheet. To accomplish this kind of task, Windows provides dialog boxes. Dialog boxes appear when you invoke a menu option that has an ellipsis (...) beside it. They resemble simplified windows, but differ in a few respects: dialog boxes have no menus (other than a Control menu), no borders, and cannot be sized.

Dialog boxes have two purposes. They display information, such as warnings, and they let you adjust the operating parameters of the program in use. The parameters you can adjust with dialog boxes range from the very simple, such as the display of a certain type of file, to the very complex—telecommunications settings, for example.

Figure I.3 shows a sample dialog box from the Windows Terminal program. This dialog box is used to configure the terminal program to operate in specific ways. It contains four of the components of a

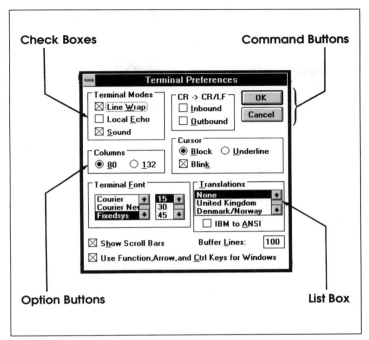

Figure I.3: The Terminal Preferences dialog box

dialog box: command buttons, check boxes, list boxes, and option buttons. These components, as well as the text boxes and drop-down list boxes that also appear in some dialog boxes, are described below.

- *Command buttons* initiate actions. The two most common command buttons are OK and Cancel. Once you have configured the options in the dialog box to your liking, you click on OK to implement your changes. Click on Cancel to return to the Windows application without making any changes. (You can invoke command buttons using keystrokes if necessary, just like menu options and menu titles. To select a command button using its mnemonic—the underlined letter in the command button—just type the mnemonic at the keyboard while holding down the Alt key.) A command button with an ellipsis (…) beside it means that the command button leads to yet another dialog box.

- A *check box* permits you to activate or inactivate individual options in a list of choices. When you select a check box, an X appears in it and the corresponding option becomes active. (Select the box again to inactivate the option.) Check boxes are not mutually exclusive; you can select more than one of them. Sometimes, you may see check box options that are dimmed. These options, like any dimmed option or button, are unavailable because of the current status of the program.

- A *list box* is a series of available choices displayed in a column. To select an item on a list, click on it. To deselect it, select another item. (To select an item using the keyboard, tap ↓ or ↑ until the item is highlighted.) If the number of items on the list exceeds the boundaries of the box, a scroll bar appears beside the list. A directory tree box, which contains a tree-shaped graphic representation of a disk's directory structure, is one kind of list box. Once you've selected a directory, the files within it usually appear in a list box adjacent to the directory tree box.

- *Option buttons,* like check boxes, permit you to activate an option in a list of choices. When you select the small hollow circle, it changes to a filled circle and the corresponding option is activated. Option buttons are different from check boxes, however, in that they designate mutually exclusive items. When you select an item, you automatically deselect any other active item. To invoke an option button, click on it. (If you are using a keyboard, press the Tab key repeatedly until the option button is highlighted and then use the arrow keys to move from button to button, highlighting each in turn. Press ↵ when the option you want is highlighted.)

- *Text boxes* allow you to specify your exact choice in an operation. For example, you might name a file you wish to delete or a font you wish to add. A text box is a rectangular

area in which you can type new information or modify
provided information. When you have specified your
choice in the text box, you can press Tab to move on to the
next component of the dialog box, or implement a dialog
box as is by pressing ↵ or clicking on OK or Yes.

• A *drop-down list box* is a list box that looks something like a
text box, but that has a small down arrow on the right
side. Click on that arrow, or press Alt-↓, and a list "drops
down." To select an item on the list, click on it, or use the
arrow keys to scroll through the items and press ↵ when
the desired item is highlighted. One kind of drop-down
list box is the drive list box. The items in this list box
are drive icons. Once a drive is selected, any adjacent
directory tree and file list boxes will change to reflect
information on the new drive.

THE MOUSE AND KEYBOARD

With its graphic icons, pull-down menus, and boxes that can be
moved or sized, the Windows interface is designed to be used with
a mouse. The keyboard should generally be reserved for entering
text and numbers in application programs. But, recognizing that a
mouse may not be available at all times, Windows provides a keystroke
alternative for every selection you can make with a mouse.

Working with the Mouse

The most basic procedure in Windows is to place the pointer over a
graphic image on-screen and then click the left mouse button. Almost everything you do in Windows consists of pointing and clicking. Clicking does three things: It selects an option, it initiates an
action, or it manipulates the screen in some way.

• *Selecting an option.* Windows often presents its user with
the option to modify Windows itself or an application running in Windows. You can set a default font, for example,
or choose the way in which files are displayed on-screen.

Windows displays lists of options and you select the ones you want by pointing and clicking. Options are usually selected using dialog boxes.

- *Initiating an action.* An integral part of Windows is the ability to initiate actions. You can direct that a program be run, you can send a document to the printer, and much more. This can be done using the keyboard, but it is often more efficient to use the mouse.

- *Manipulating the screen.* Windows programs can appear on-screen simultaneously, sometimes overlapping and obscuring each other. Using the mouse, you can size program windows and make them smaller or larger, or temporarily hide them.

By default, the right mouse button goes unused by Windows, but some Windows application programs rely on it extensively. (If you wish, you can make the right mouse button the active button; see "Swapping Mouse Buttons" in Part II.) How it functions is determined by the software in use.

Another common mouse technique is *double-clicking.* Almost every option you can select in Windows has a default action associated with it; click twice in rapid succession on the option to initiate that default action. For example, you might want to open a file from inside a word processor. If you are presented with a list of files, the normal procedure would be to find the desired file on the list, select it, then click on the OK command button. The shortcut is to place the pointer over the name of the file you wish to open, and then double-click; the file will load.

The pointer is often used to manipulate objects on-screen, both moving them and sizing them. To move an object, you usually place the pointer on it, then click and hold the left mouse button. This "grabs" the object. Then you can move the object wherever you want. The process is very similar for sizing, except that you usually grab and move a border or box surrounding some object. (The mouse pointer becomes a double-headed arrow when resizing.) The process of clicking, holding, and moving is called *dragging.*

Table I.1 presents a summary of the terms used for mouse commands throughout the rest of this reference guide.

Table I.1: Mouse commands

Term	Meaning
Click on or select an option	Place the pointer over the option and click the left mouse button.
Double-click	Click on an option twice in rapid succession, invoking its default action or state.
Pull down a menu	Click on the menu option, allowing the menu to drop down.
Drag	Click on an object, hold the mouse button down, and move the object to a desired location.

Working with the Keyboard

Windows is designed to be used with a mouse. However, you can use a keyboard to do almost anything in Windows that a mouse can do.

Navigating the menu systems in Windows programs is very easy to do using the keyboard. Most menu items have a single underlined letter in their name. That letter is called a *mnemonic*. The mnemonic denotes the key you need to press in conjunction with the Alt key to make the menu drop down. For example, the mnemonic for the File Manager's Options menu is *O*. With the File Manager on the screen, press Alt-O, and the Options menu will drop down.

Once a menu has been pulled down, you can use mnemonics alone to invoke menu options; you don't have to use the Alt key anymore. So, to select Minimize on Use from the Options menu, you would

Table I.2: Keyboard commands for standard Windows procedures

Action	Key Sequence
Pull down Control menu in group window	Alt-Hyphen
Pull down Control menu in document window	Alt-Spacebar
Move between items in a dialog box	Tab (Shift-Tab moves backwards)
Select or deselect a check box or option button	Spacebar
Move through a list	↑ or ↓
Move through a list rapidly	PgUp or PgDn
Pull down a drop-down list box	Alt-↓
Select OK command button	↵
Select Cancel command button	Esc

first pull down the menu by pressing Alt-O, then select Minimize on Use by simply typing M.

Mnemonics are also widely used in dialog boxes. With the dialog box on the screen, you simply press Tab to move between dialog box components; to move backward, press Shift-Tab. Press Spacebar to select or deselect the item you want. Alternatively, you can press Alt plus the mnemonic key for the option you wish to select.

Anything you can select or deselect with a mouse, you can select or deselect with the keyboard. Table I.2 describes how to perform standard Windows procedures with the keyboard.

THE WINDOWS PROGRAMS

The remainder of this section provides a short description of each program supplied with Windows. Some of these programs, such as the Program Manager and the Print Manager, are vital parts of Windows and must be used if you are to operate the environment. Others are simply underpowered versions of commercially available applications, provided by Microsoft both to add value to Windows and to act as examples of how a Windows program should operate. The following paragraphs present the programs in the order of their relative importance.

These descriptions are meant only to familiarize you with the Windows programs. Detailed instructions for the operations you can perform with these programs appear in Part II, an alphabetical guide to the features and operations of Windows. Consult the index or the table of contents to find the exact entry you need.

THE PROGRAM MANAGER

The Program Manager is the Windows utility that runs applications. It starts automatically when you run Windows, and exiting (or *closing*) it is the only way to leave Windows.

When you run Windows for the first time, the Program Manager appears on-screen, as shown in Figure I.4. Within the primary Program Manager window, there are secondary windows called *group windows*. They appear on-screen as fully opened windows, such as the one titled "Main" in Figure I.4, or as *group icons,* which are located below the Main window in the same figure. A group icon is a group window that has been minimized.

Group windows carry with them the limitations of all document windows: they cannot be sized or moved outside the confines of the Program Manager application window. Group windows organize programs into discrete, related sets. One group window, for example, may contain all programs associated with word processing,

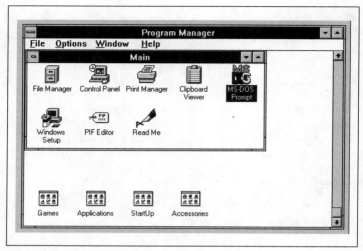

Figure I.4: The Program Manager

while another may be for telecommunications. Windows comes with five default group windows: Main, Accessories, StartUp, Applications, and Games. You may have chosen to install other group windows, as well.

When a group window is open, the icons for the programs you can run are displayed. You can maximize or minimize group windows, add programs to them, delete programs from them, and move or copy programs between them.

Like group windows, group icons cannot be moved outside the Program Manager window. Group icons appear as rectangles containing small icons.

Within each group window are program icons that represent individual application programs. By selecting a program icon, you can run the program it represents. Program icons can be moved between program groups, copied, or renamed. They can also be configured to execute in unique ways, to suit your individual needs. For example, a program icon might automatically run your word processor and open a specific memorandum or report.

See Also   Part II: Application Programs, Program Groups and
Group Windows, Standard Operations

THE FILE MANAGER

Both Windows 3.0 and Windows 3.1 provide a program for
manipulating files, called the File Manager, which presents you
with a visual representation of all the disks and files in your system.
When the File Manager runs, a window similar to the one in Figure I.5 appears.

As you can see, the File Manager uses document windows (see "The
Windows Interface"). The directory structure for the hard disk, and a
list of files in the current directory, appear in a document window
called a *directory window*. From a directory window, you can select one

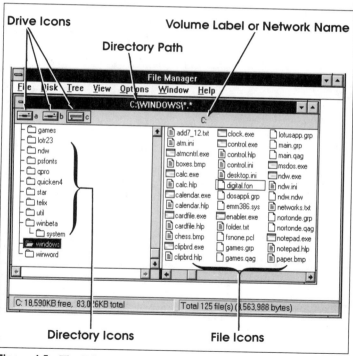

Figure I.5: The File Manager

Table I.3: : Components of the File Manager

Component	Description
Drive icons	Denote the available drives. Click on a drive icon to log onto the drive.
Directory path	Always appears in directory window title bar. Specifies the path of the current directory for that window.
Directory icons	Symbolize directories within a tree structure; in the contents list (the list of files), directory icons denote subdirectories beneath the current directory.
Volume label or network name	Specifies volume label of currently logged disk drive or, on a network, the network name.
File icons	Can represent program files and document files; there is a generic icon for all other types of files. Located next to file names in the contents list.
Up icon	In the contents list, an up icon denotes the directory above the current directory. Double-click on the up icon to move to that directory.

or more files and change their attributes; move them between directories; or open, print, rename, delete, or copy them.

Table I.3 describes the various components of the files Manager.

See Also   Part II: File and Directory Management

WINDOWS HELP

To aid you in understanding and using Windows, Microsoft has provided one of the most advanced help facilities available, called simply Windows Help. Help does not appear as a program icon in a group window. Instead, Windows Help is accessible at any time from within almost every Windows program.

Windows Help is always used in conjunction with an application-specific Help text file supplied by the application developer. Most Windows Help files are divided into four general sections:

- Contents
- Search for Help on
- How to Use Help
- About *program name*

The first of these, Contents, is further divided into the subsections How To, Commands, and Keyboard.

The Windows Help screen is divided into two parts. The upper portion of the screen contains a set of *navigation buttons,* which aid you in moving through the Help text; see Figure I.6. The lower portion displays Help's explanatory text.

See Also   Part II: The Help System

THE CLIPBOARD

The Windows Clipboard is a temporary storage location for text or graphics. Using the Cut, Copy, or Paste menu options in a Windows application program's Edit menu, you can transfer data from any program into the Clipboard and then copy that data into a different program. (Those programs that don't have an Edit menu, such as Windows Clock, are so simple that they don't need access to the Clipboard.)

You can also cut or paste text (but not graphics) from DOS applications into the Clipboard. If the DOS program is running in full-screen mode, however, you must copy the full screen into the Clipboard.

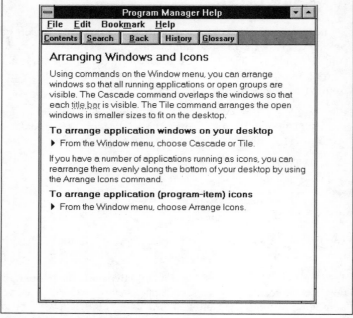

Figure I.6: A standard Help screen

Clipboard Viewer, located in the Main group, allows you to view and delete any Clipboard data. Using the Clipboard Viewer, you can save the contents of the Clipboard to file and retrieve them later.

See Also   Part II: Clipboard Operations

THE OBJECT PACKAGER

The Object Packager is a program that helps you use Windows object linking and embedding (OLE) facilities. Using OLE, you can paste—embed—information from one Windows program into another.

You are not restricted to embedding data, however. You can also embed icons that represent the data. That's where the Object Packager comes in—it takes the data currently in the Clipboard and assigns to it any icon you choose. Once the data is "packaged" in the icon, you can paste the icon into your target application.

See Also   Appendix: Object Linking and Embedding

THE SETUP PROGRAM

Setup allows you to reconfigure Windows for a new type of display, keyboard, mouse, or local area network (LAN). In the process, you will need to insert some of the original Windows installation disks in the computer's floppy-disk drive, so keep the disks handy. When you are done, you must exit Windows and then restart it for the change to take effect.

THE CONTROL PANEL

The Control Panel is your tool for configuring Windows. Use it to change the default printer and printer port, install a new printer driver, install new fonts, customize the mouse, or change the time and date. You can also permanently change the colors that Windows uses, or use a graphic image generated in Paintbrush as a backdrop for the Windows desktop.

THE PRINT MANAGER

The Print Manager automatically manages all printing done by Windows applications. When you direct a Windows application to print information, the application formats the information for the default printer and stores it in a *print file*. The print file is then passed on to the Print Manager.

See Also   Part II: Print Manager Operations

THE MACRO RECORDER

The Macro Recorder is a program in the Accessories group that records keystrokes and mouse movements and plays them back at a later time. Using the Macro Recorder you can make a record, called a *macro*, of any often-used mouse movements or key sequences. Then,

22 The Windows Programs

whenever you require that series of actions, you can play the macro back with a single keystroke.

THE PIF EDITOR

The PIF Editor is a Windows accessory program that creates, edits, and saves PIF files. PIF is an acronym for *program information file*. A PIF file (while redundant, the term is in common usage) contains information that Windows uses to run a standard DOS application. It tells Windows what the program's name is, what kind of video it uses, how much memory it requires, what ports it accesses, and more. (Each non-Windows application should have its own PIF file.)

See Also   Part II: PIF Editor Operations

MICROSOFT WRITE

Microsoft Write is a word processor supplied with Windows. Although it is not as powerful as Microsoft Word, Write performs all necessary word processing functions, such as block copying, moving, and deleting. It creates and manipulates italic, superscript, subscript, boldfaced, and underlined text. Write also has undo and search and replace functions.

NOTEPAD

Notepad is an ASCII (American Standard Code for Information Interchange) text editor. That is, it is a rudimentary word processor that works only with text files in the ASCII format. Because such files contain none of the formatting information normally found in word processor files, you cannot use Notepad to boldface or italicize text, assign fonts, or the like. Notepad *is* useful for writing quick notes and memos, creating and editing batch files, and editing the system configuration files, CONFIG.SYS and AUTOEXEC.BAT.

See Also   Part II: Notepad Operations

PAINTBRUSH

Paintbrush is a drawing program for use with Windows. The Paintbrush toolbox, which is displayed on-screen, contains 18 drawing tools that can be used to produce and manipulate basic shapes. Using Paintbrush, you can create, save, modify, and print detailed color or black-and-white graphic images.

WINDOWS TERMINAL

Terminal is a Windows application that allows your computer to exchange information with other computers via telephone connections. Using a computer peripheral called a modem, which connects to your serial port and then to the telephone system, Terminal can access information services like CompuServe or MCI Mail.

See Also   Part II: Terminal Communications

CARDFILE

Windows Cardfile is designed to replace the standard business Rolodex file found on many desks. It is a limited-use, flat-file database program that lets you create "index cards" on-screen, sort them, view them, and use them to automatically dial a telephone number printed on the card.

See Also   Part II: Cardfile Operations

CALENDAR

Windows Calendar is a combination monthly calendar and daily appointment book program. You can use Calendar to keep track of appointments, vacations, paydays, holidays, and more. It displays time in two ways: as a monthly calendar, called the Month view, and as a list of daily appointments, called the Day view.

See Also   Part II: Calendar Operations

CALCULATOR

The Calculator accessory program imitates both standard (algebraic) and scientific hand-held calculators. In Standard mode, it
performs addition, subtraction, multiplication, and division;
it derives square roots, percentages, and reciprocals; and has
memory storage and recall features. In Scientific mode, it performs
hexadecimal, decimal, octal, and binary calculations; it also has
statistical, logarithmic, exponential, and logical functions.

See Also   Part II: Calculator Operations

CLOCK

Another accessory program included with Windows is Clock, which
provides an on-screen timepiece. When minimized to an icon, Clock
continues to keep the correct time and displays it in the icon. Since
Clock uses only about 12K of memory, it's as efficient to keep a
timepiece on your Windows desktop as it is to keep a physical clock on
your real desktop.

See Also   Part II: The Clock Utility

CHARACTER MAP

The Character Map is a Windows 3.1 utility program designed to
simplify access to special characters not directly available on a keyboard, such as foreign currency symbols, Greek letters, and
trademark and currency symbols. Until now, to use one of these
characters you've had to look up an arbitrary three-digit ASCII
code and (holding down the Alt key) type that number into your
document. You may also have had to switch between fonts or character sets to find the character. The Character Map utility displays a
grid of all the characters in a font you've chosen; you select one and
then paste it via the Clipboard into a Windows application.

See Also   Part II: Character Map Operations Utility

Part II

Alphabetical Guide to Features and Operations

APPLICATION PROGRAMS

The following pages present, in alphabetical order, the operations you can perform upon application programs within the Windows environment: arranging application icons, associating an application with its file types, installing an application, running an application, terminating an application, and tiling and cascading application windows. See the appropriate entries under "Standard Operations" for those tasks performed within application programs that are common to all Windows programs.

ARRANGING APPLICATION ICONS

In Windows, sometimes the application icons may be scattered all over the desktop, making it easy for them to be hidden by windows. Using Task List, you can arrange all the application icons in one neat row at the bottom of the desktop.

1. Invoke Task List by pressing Ctrl-Esc, or by double-clicking anywhere on the Windows desktop. Task List will appear, with a list box of the currently executing applications within it.

2. Select Arrange Icons (Alt-A). Task List will disappear, and all the application icons will appear at the bottom of the desktop.

ASSOCIATING FILE TYPES WITH APPLICATIONS

To associate a file is to link all files with a specific extension to a specific program file. If you are using MultiMate, for instance, you can tell File Manager that all files that end in .DOC (which is the file extension for MultiMate documents) should be associated with the program file WP.EXE. From that point on, when you open or double-click on any .DOC file, MultiMate will automatically run and load the associated program file. Using the File Manager you can create and delete associations.

1. Select the file whose extension you wish to associate.

2. Pull down the File menu (Alt-F) and select Associate (A). The Associate dialog box will appear.

3. From the Associate With drop-down list box, select the Windows program with which you wish to associate the file type. Or, if you are associating the file type with a DOS application, click on the Browse button (Alt-B) to browse through the drives in your system and find the DOS program. Once you find the program file, double-click on it. The Associate dialog box will reappear.

4. Click on OK or press ↵.

Notes It is important to key in the complete path name and program file name. For example, if the program file were MultiMate's (WP.EXE), and it resided in the WPROC directory of the C drive, you would type C:\WPROC\WP.EXE.

The Associate With list box contains the names of all Windows programs. Some Windows programs register their file types with Windows—they let Windows know what types of files they use. If the file type you are associating works with one of these programs, you can simply select from the list of Windows programs presented here.

You can also associate a new file type with a listed Windows program. For example, you might have renamed Windows Write documents from their default extension of .WRI to .ACT, for the accounting department, or .JOE to indicate that a group of documents were written by Joe. You can associate .ACT or .JOE with Windows Write files by first typing the new extension in the Files With Extension text box, then using the Associate With list box.

INSTALLING A NEW PROGRAM

The method for installing a new program differs from program to program. The installation procedure for Word for Windows, for example, is not the same as that for Ami Pro. There is no definitive method for installing a new program. However, there are some general rules to follow.

The installation procedure for most Windows programs involves using a set of installation disks and running a program called INSTALL.EXE, located on the first of those disks. There are several ways to run a program located on a floppy. One way involves the use of the Windows File Manager program and is described in the section titled "Running an Application from the File Manager." Another method requires the use of the Program Manager and is described below.

1. With the Program Manager window on-screen and active, pull down the File menu (Alt-F) and select Run (R). A dialog box appears, prompting you for the path and name of the program to run.

2. Type **A:\INSTALL** and click on OK or press ↵. This starts the installation program.

RUNNING AN APPLICATION PROGRAM

You run an application in Windows by selecting the application's icon in one of the Program Manager's group windows, then selecting the option to run it. For an explanation of the Program Manager, see "The Program Manager" in Part I.

1. Open the Group window containing the icon of the program you wish to run.

2. Using the direction keys, highlight the icon of the program you wish to run, and press ↵.
    or
    Double-click the mouse pointer on the icon of the program you wish to run. When you double-click on an icon, the program will run right away.

An alternative method is to use the Program Manager's menu system to run a program:

1. Select the icon of the program you wish to run by placing the mouse pointer on it and clicking once.

2. Pull down the File menu.

3. Select Open. The program associated with the icon you selected will run.

See Also Running an Application from the File Manager

Running an Application
Using the Run Menu Option

The Program Manager has a special Run menu option that is usually used to run uninstalled programs from floppy disks. Most of the
programs that fall into this category are installation programs
themselves. (See "Installing a New Program.") It is also sometimes
useful, however, to use the Program Manager's Run option to execute a program on one-time basis. (If you are going to be running
the program frequently, it makes sense to add it to one of the Program Manager's group windows. See "Adding a Program to a
Group.") The procedure for using the Run option is as follows:

1. With the Program Manager window on-screen and active,
   pull down the File menu (Alt-F) and select Run (R). A
   dialog box that prompts you for the path and file name of
   the program to run will appear.

2. Type the path and file name of the program you wish to
   run. If you don't know the name or location of the program, click on the Browse command button. The resulting
   dialog box allows you to inspect the drives in your system
   and select the program you want to execute. Use the drive
   list box to change the current disk drive, if necessary; use
   the directory tree box to navigate the current drive's directory structure. Select the program you wish to execute by
   clicking on its file name in the list box on the left side of
   the dialog box.

3. Once you have either typed a name or selected it via the
   Browse dialog box, click on OK or press ↵ to run the
   program.

Notes   You can also use the File Manager to run a program. See
"Running an Application from the File Manager."

Running an
Application from the File Manager

The File Manager is not just a tool for organizing and copying files:
you can also use it to run programs. Windows treats four file types
as programs: those with .PIF, .EXE, .COM, and .BAT extensions.

1. From the directory pane of the File Manager window, select the directory containing the program file you wish to run. A list of the files in the selected directory appears in the file list pane (on the right side of the screen).

2. Place the mouse pointer over the program's file name and double-click, or use the Tab and direction keys to select the file and press ↵.

Notes   If the program file you have selected is a DOS program, it will run in full-screen mode.

See Also   Creating a Program Icon

TERMINATING A DOS APPLICATION

Sometimes DOS applications malfunction when they run under Windows. This is especially true of older DOS applications and ones that directly try to control the display adaptor or hard disk. When a DOS application will no longer respond to keyboard or mouse input of any kind, and you cannot close it by selecting End Task from Task List, you can choose to terminate it. This is done by switching from the application to the Windows desktop, then using the application's Control menu to select the Terminate option.

Once a DOS program has been terminated, there is a distinct possibility that Windows could become unstable. Before you terminate a program, it is strongly advised that you close all active windows. Once the program is terminated, exit Windows and reboot your computer.

Steps Using the Mouse

1. With the malfunctioning DOS program on the screen, press Alt-Esc to switch back to the Windows desktop.

2. Close all executing Windows programs. When prompted, save the open data files of each program to disk.

3. Click the control button of the malfunctioning DOS program; its Control menu will appear.

4. Select Settings. A dialog box will appear. This box allows you to adjust various settings for DOS programs that execute under Windows.

5. Select Terminate. You will see a warning dialog box that advises you to reboot your computer once you have terminated the application.

6. Select OK.

Steps Using the Keyboard

1. With the malfunctioning DOS program on the screen, press Alt-Esc to switch back to the Windows desktop.

2. Close all executing Windows programs. When prompted, save the open data files of each program to disk.

3. Press Alt-Esc until the title bar of the malfunctioning DOS program is highlighted.

4. Press Alt-Spacebar. The program's Control menu will appear.

5. Select Settings by typing **T**. A dialog box will appear. This box allows you to adjust various settings for DOS programs that execute under Windows.

6. Select Terminate by typing **T**. You will see a warning dialog box that advises you to reboot your computer once you have terminated the application.

7. Press Tab to highlight the OK button, then press ↵.

TILING AND CASCADING APPLICATION WINDOWS

If you open more than two application windows at a time, the Windows desktop can get crowded and it becomes difficult to see which windows are open. To solve this problem, the Task List utility has two commands, Cascade Windows and Tile Windows, that automatically size and place application windows.

When open applications are displayed in a cascade, they overlap each other. Only one window is visible—the one that was active when Cascade was selected (see Figure II.1).

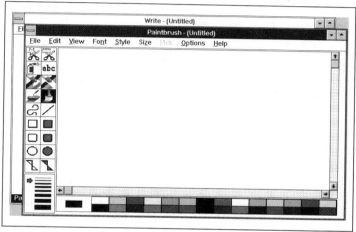

Figure II.1: Application windows in a cascade file

When open application windows are tiled, the space on the Windows desktop is evenly divided among the windows; they are arranged on the screen so they don't overlap. At least some portion of the program area of each group is visible (see Figure II.2).

Before selecting either Cascade Windows or Tile Windows, make sure the windows you want to arrange are open.

See Also   Programs Groups and Group Windows

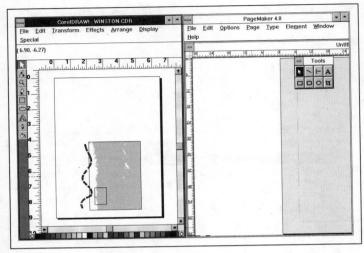

Figure II.2: Tiled application windows

Cascading Windows

1. Invoke Task List by pressing Ctrl-Esc, or by double-
    clicking anywhere on the Windows desktop. Task
    List will appear, displaying a list box of the cur-
    rently executing applications.

2. Select Cascade (Alt-C). Task List will disappear, and all
    open application windows will appear in a cascade.

Tiling Windows

1. Invoke Task List by pressing Ctrl-Esc, or by double-click-
    ing anywhere on the Windows desktop. Task List will ap-
    pear, displaying a list box of the currently executing
    applications.

2. Select Tile (Alt-T). Task List will disappear, and all open
    application windows will appear tiled.

CALCULATOR OPERATIONS

The Calculator program imitates both standard (algebraic) and scientific hand-held calculators.

In Standard mode, Calculator performs addition, subtraction, multiplication, and division; it derives square roots, percentages, and reciprocals; it also has memory storage and recall features. In Scientific mode, Calculator performs hexadecimal, decimal, octal, and binary math; it also has statistical, logarithmic, exponential, and logical functions.

The Calculator icon appears in the Accessories program group. To start Calculator, follow these steps:

1. Open the Accessories program group.

2. Double-click on the Calculator icon, or use the direction keys to highlight the icon and press ↵. The Calculator window appears, in whatever mode it was in last. (The default mode is Standard.)

CHANGING TO THE SCIENTIFIC CALCULATOR

The scientific calculator is useful for people doing programming, statistical mathematics, or advanced algebra.

*   Pull down the View menu (Alt-V) and select Scientific (S). The scientific calculator will appear.

RETURNING TO THE STANDARD CALCULATOR

Follow these instructions if you have previous set the Calculator for the Scientific mode and now want to return to the Standard mode:

*   Pull down the View menu (Alt-V) and select Standard (T).

CALENDAR OPERATIONS

Windows Calendar is a combination monthly calendar and daily appointment book program. You can use Calendar to keep track of appointments, vacations, paydays, holidays, and more. Calendar displays time in two ways: as a monthly calendar, called the Month view, and as a list of daily appointments, called the Day view. The Day view display is pictured in Figure II.3.

The horizontal scroll arrows on the date and time line in the Day view move you through the appointment list in one-day increments; when the Month view is displayed, the arrows move you through the calendar in one-month increments. The vertical scroll arrows in the Day view move the cursor up and down in one-hour increments.

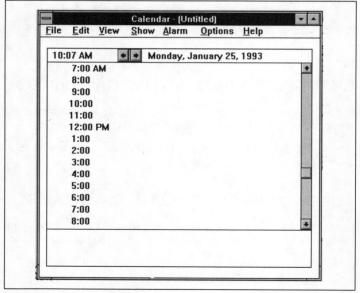

Figure II.3: The Day view screen

You can also use Calendar to remind you of appointments with an alarm. You can configure the program to display the hours and minutes in various ways.

The Calendar icon appears in the Accessories program group. To start Calendar, follow these steps:

1. Open the Accessories program group.

2. Double-click on the Calendar icon, or move to the icon using the direction keys and press ↵. The Calendar window will appear, with the daily appointment list displayed in its workspace.

ADDING OR DELETING A SPECIAL TIME

A special time is a time that is not usually displayed in the Day view because it does not fall on the hour, half-hour, or quarter-hour. If you have an appointment at a special time, Calendar will insert the time in the Day view, allowing you to list the appointment. Special times can be inserted for individual days only; you can't automatically make a special time appear on all days. The Special Time option is not available in the Month view.

To Add a Special Time

1. Use the shortcut key F7, or pull down the Options menu (Alt-O) and select Special Time (S). A dialog box will appear.

2. Type the special time in the Special Time text box. Be sure to separate the hours and minutes with a colon.

3. Click on the Insert command button or press Alt-I. The special time will appear in the appointment list.

To Delete a Special Time

1. In the Day view appointment list, click on the special time you wish to delete or move to it using the direction keys.

2. Use the shortcut key F7, or pull down the Options menu (Alt-O) and select Special Time (S). A dialog box will appear with the special time displayed in the text box.

3. Click on the Delete command button or press Alt-D. The special time will be deleted from the appointment list.

CHANGING THE HOUR/MINUTE DISPLAY

Calendar lets you change the time scale displayed in the Day view. You can make and display appointments for times on the hour, half-hour, or quarter-hour. You can also specify the starting time for each daily appointment list, and change the display from the 12-hour clock to the 24-hour clock used by the military.

1. Pull down the Options menu (Alt-O) and select Day Settings (D). A dialog box containing two sets of option buttons and a text box will appear.

2. Set the interval at which you want times displayed by selecting one of the Interval option buttons.

3. Change the hour format by selecting one of the Hour Format option buttons.

4. To change the starting time for the daily appointment list, click on the Starting Time text box, or press the Tab key repeatedly until the Starting Time text box is highlighted, and then key in the time. Make sure to use a colon to separate the hours and minutes.

5. Click on OK or press ↵.

CHANGING THE VIEW

Calendar displays time in two ways: as a monthly calendar and as a list of daily appointments. Instructions for toggling between the two are given below:

• You can toggle quickly between the daily and monthly views by double-clicking on the date in the status line.

or

• Starting from the Day (appointment list) view, pull down the View menu (Alt-V) and select Month (M). The display will change to a monthly calendar. To toggle back to the Day view, pull down the View menu and click on Day (D).

Notes   There are shortcut keys for the steps above . Press F9 to switch to the Month view. Press F8 to switch to the Day view.

ENTERING AN APPOINTMENT

Calendar allows you to enter an appointment in the displayed appointment list at any time. (To control how time is displayed—by hour, half-hour, quarter-hour—see "Changing Hour/Minute Display.")

1.   Starting from the Day (appointment list) view, move the mouse pointer into the appointment area, directly to the right of the appointment time, and click. A blinking, upright cursor will appear adjacent to the time.

2.   Type text describing the appointment.

3.   Press ⏎ to move to the next available appointment time, or repeat step 1.

SETTING AN ALARM

Calendar will set an alarm to inform you of an appointment. If Calendar is active and on-screen, the alarm will take the form of a message box. Click OK or press ⏎ to remove the message from the screen. If Calendar is inactive and on-screen, its title bar will flash. If Calendar is an icon, the icon will flash. Click on the icon or the Calendar window, then click on OK or press ⏎ to acknowledge the alarm. In all cases, if you have the beep set to on, four beeps will sound when the alarm goes off.

1.   Starting from the Day (appointment list) view, move the mouse pointer to the appointment for which you wish to set an alarm and click, or move to the appointment using the direction keys and press ⏎. A vertical, blinking cursor will appear in the appointment text.

2.   Use the shortcut key F5, or pull down the Alarm (Alt-A) menu and click on Set (S). A figure of a bell will appear beside the specified time to indicate that the alarm has been set.

Setting Early Alarm Ring

Once an alarm has been set, you have the option of customizing it so that it beeps up to ten minutes before the appointment, allowing you time to prepare. You can also specify that no beep sounds when the alarm goes off, which means that you will have only a visual indication of the alarm.

1.   Set an alarm. (See "Setting an Alarm.")

2.   Pull down the Alarm menu (Alt-A) and select Controls (C). A dialog box containing a text box and a check box will appear.

3.   Determine how many minutes before the appointment you want the alarm to ring (you can choose from 1 through 10) and key this number into the Early Ring text box.

4.   If you like, deselect the Sound check box and the alarm will make no sound.

5.   Click on OK or press ↵.

SHOWING DAYS AND MONTHS

Calendar can show you the next or previous daily schedule in Day view or the next or previous monthly calendar in Month view. Calendar will also display the schedule or calendar for any day you specify, as long as the date is from the range January 1, 1980 through December 31, 2099.

To Show a Sequential Day or Month

•   Pull down the Show (Alt-S) menu and select Previous (P) or Next (N), depending on which schedule or calendar you want to view. You can also move to the previous schedule or calendar by pressing Ctrl-PgUp. To move to the next schedule or calendar, press Ctrl-PgDn.

To Show a Specific Day

1. Pull down the Show menu (Alt-S) and select Date (D), or press F4. A dialog box will appear, asking you to key in the date you wish to show.

2. Type in the date using one of three formats: dd/mm/yy, dd-mm-yy, or dd/mm/yyyy.

3. Click on OK or press ↵.

Notes To return to today's date, pull down the Show menu (Alt-S) and select Today (T).

You must key in the data using the date format selected on the International settings in Control Panel. In any format, if you truncate the year to the last two digits, Windows will assume you mean the twentieth century, not the twenty-first (1990, for example, not 2090).

Marking a Day

When you use Calendar in the Month view, you can mark individual days with one of five symbols to represent the specific type of day—holiday, payday, etc.—for easier reference.

1. Starting with Calendar in the Month view, select the day you wish to mark.

2. Use the shortcut key F6, or pull down the Options menu (Alt-O) and select Mark (M). The Day Markings dialog box will appear. It has a check box for each of the five symbols: square brackets, parentheses, a lowercase "o," a lowercase "x," and an underline.

3. Select the desired symbol by using the mouse, or press Tab to move among the check boxes and press the Spacebar to make your selection. You can select more than one symbol.

4. Click on OK or press ↵.

CARDFILE OPERATIONS

Windows Cardfile is a limited-use, flat-file database program that imitates a desktop Rolodex. You can create "index cards" on-screen, sort them, view them, and use them to automatically dial a telephone number.

The standard Cardfile screen is composed of three parts (see Figure II.4):

- The *status line* tells you what type of view is in effect and how many cards are in the current card file. The status line also contains scroll arrows; the left arrow moves you backward through the cards and the right arrow moves you forward.

- The *index line* holds text, and is the sort key Cardfile uses to automatically alphabetize the entire card file. You can type anything you want here, but if you are using Cardfile as a Rolodex, it's probably wise to type a last name and first name.

- The *information area* is where you type the information you want on the card.

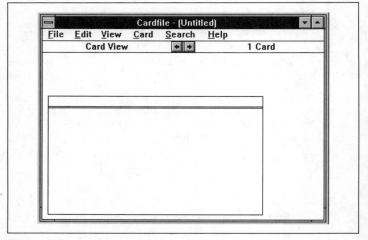

Figure II.4: A standard Cardfile screen

The Cardfile icon appears in the Accessories program group. To start Cardfile, follow these steps:

1. Open the Accessories program group.

2. Double-click on the Cardfile icon, or move to the icon using the direction keys and press ↵. The Cardfile window will appear with a blank card displayed in its workspace.

ADDING A CARD

As you use Cardfile, you will probably need to add new cards to your file. Follow these steps:

1. Pull down the Card menu (Alt-C) and select Add (A), or press F7. The Add dialog box will appear. (Though there is nothing to indicate it, this is where Cardfile expects you to key in the index line for the new card.)

2. Type the index text (usually a last name and a first name), then click on OK or press ↵. The Cardfile window will reappear with the new card at the forefront. There will be a blinking vertical cursor in the upper-left corner of the in-formation area.

3. Type the information you want on the card.

See Also   Creating/Editing a Card

AUTODIALING

If your computer is attached to a standard Hayes or Hayes-compatible modem, Cardfile can use the telephone number listed in the informa-tion area to dial your telephone. The autodial feature of Cardfile scans the text in a card and uses the first number it finds as the telephone number—make sure that the first number that appears on a card is the phone number, or type the phone number in the Number text box con-tained in the Autodial dialog box.

1. Start by making sure that the card containing the number you wish to dial is at the top of the card stack. Pull down the Card menu (Alt-C) and select Autodial (T), or press F5. The Autodial dialog box will appear.

2. If you have autodialed previously, go to step 4. If you are autodialing for the first time, click on the Setup command button or press Alt-S. The Autodial dialog box will expand and display option buttons for telling Cardfile the baud rate of the modem, the type of dialing the phone uses, and the serial port in use.

3. Configure each of these settings to match your system.

4. Click on OK or press ↵.

Notes The Autodial feature supports system-specific prefixes and can, for example, dial 9 from an office to get an outside line (to do this, type the desired prefix and toggle the Use Prefix option on). However, it has no way of knowing if it is dialing a long-distance or local number. If you are required to dial 1 before dialing a long-distance number, make sure that 1 prefaces the number. A local number on a card might read "555-1234," while a long-distance number would read "1-404-555-1234."

CHANGING THE CARD VIEW

Cardfile offers two ways for you to view a card file: the Card view and the List view. In the Card view, you are looking at a stack of index cards, with one card fully visible on the top of the stack and only the index lines of the other cards visible. In the List view, the index lines of the cards are presented in list format, but none of the information on the cards is displayed. The List view comes in handy when you have a great many cards and you need to look through them quickly.

1. Pull down the View menu (Alt-V) and select List (L). The Cardfile workspace will change to a list of the index lines on all the cards.

2. Click on the index line of the card you wish to see or move to it using the direction keys.

3. Pull down the View menu (Alt-V) and select Card (C). Cardfile will switch back to the Card view, and the selected card will be at the top of the stack.

CONFIGURING CARDFILE
FOR PASTING TEXT AND GRAPHICS

You can paste both text and graphic images into a Cardfile card if you configure Cardfile to receive this material before you begin a paste or a paste-link operation.

Cardfile is one of the Windows accessory programs that use Windows object linking and embedding (OLE) technology. (For an in-depth explanation of OLE, see the Appendix.) Using OLE, you can embed a graphic image in a Cardfile card, and then later direct the application that generated it to automatically run and load that image by simply double-clicking on the image. You can then edit it. When you close the editing application, the graphic in Cardfile will be updated. You can also use OLE to directly link to file on disk, as explained in "Paste-Linking Text or Graphics into Cardfile."

By default, Cardfile accepts textual information only. You must select a menu option to configure the program to accept graphics.

• Pull down the Edit menu (Alt-E) and select Picture (E). You can now paste graphic images into Cardfile. Pull down the Edit menu again and select Text (X) to reconfigure Cardfile to accept text.

CREATING/EDITING A CARD

When Cardfile first runs, there is a blank card visible in its workspace.

1. Double-click on the card's index line or press F6. A dialog box prompting you to key in the index text will appear.

2. Type the index text (usually a last name and a first name), then click on OK or press ↵. The Cardfile window will reappear. There will be a blinking vertical cursor in the upper-left corner of the information area.

3. Type the information you want on the card. You may want to follow the standard convention for typing a name and address here, with one exception: if you intend to autodial directly from the card, make sure you type the phone number *before* the street number, zip code, or any other number.

That's because when Cardfile autodials, it searches the information area for the first number it finds and then uses it as the telephone number. (Of course, if you enter the phone number in the Autodial dialog box, you need not follow this format.)

DELETING A CARD

A card file can become crowded with outdated names and addresses; you will sometimes need to delete a card. Follow these steps:

1. Bring the card you wish to delete to the front of the stack by clicking in its index line, or press PgDn repeatedly until the card comes to the front of the stack.

2. Pull down the Card menu (Alt-C) and select Delete (D). A dialog box will appear, asking you to confirm the deletion.

3. Click on OK or press ⌐. The card will be deleted.

DUPLICATING A CARD

You can copy exact information from a selected card to a new card.

1. Bring the card you wish to copy to the front of the stack by clicking in its index line, or press PgDn until the card comes to the front of the stack.

2. Pull down the Card menu (Alt-C) and select Duplicate (P). A new card with the exact contents of the selected card will be added to the card file.

FINDING TEXT

Cardfile will search all the cards in a card file for any text you specify. Note, however, that Cardfile searches for the text on only the cards themselves, not on the index lines, and that it does not differentiate between whole words and parts of words.

1. Pull down the Search menu (Alt-S) and select Find (F). A dialog box will appear, asking you to key in the text for which you wish to search.

2. Type the text you wish to search for, then click on Find
    Next or press ↵. Cardfile will find the first occurrence of
    the specified text. You can continue searching through the
    file for the same text by clicking on Find Next or pressing
    ↵ again. When you reach the card you are searching for,
    click on Cancel or press Esc.

MERGING CARD FILES

Cardfile lets you merge two card files into a single file. Follow these
instructions:

1. Open one of the files to be merged.

2. Pull down the File menu (Alt-F) and select Merge (M). A
    dialog box will appear, containing a list of the available
    card files.

3. Double-click on the name of the card file you wish to
    merge into the open file. Or, Type the name of the card file
    you wish to merge into the open file, or select the file's
    name from the list box. Click on OK or press ↵.

OPENING A CARD FILE

Before Cardfile can work with previously created card files, they
must be loaded into Cardfile from disk. Complete these steps:

1. Pull down the File menu (Alt-F) and select Open (O).
    A dialog box listing the available card files will appear.

2. Double-click on the name of the card file to load or, type
    the name of the card file to load, or click on its name in the
    list box. Click on OK or press ↵.

PASTING TEXT OR GRAPHICS INTO CARDFILE

1. Make sure the text or graphic you want to paste is in
    the Clipboard, then place the cursor at the point on the
    card where you wish the pasted material to appear.

2. To specific that you want to paste text, pull down
    Cardfile's Edit menu (Alt-E) and select Text (X). To

specify a graphic, pull down the Edit menu (Alt-E)
and select Picture (E).

3. Pull down Cardfile's Edit menu (Alt-E) and select Paste
(P), or press Ctrl-V.

Paste-Linking Text or Graphics into Cardfile

When using the linking portion of OLE, you define a link between two data files—one you are currently working on and
another that is stored on disk and/or is being used by a different
program. For example, you may use Paintbrush to display a
graphic image and then copy that image into the Clipboard.
Using OLE, you can establish a link between Cardfile and the
file that contains that image. When you edit the image in
Paintbrush, the image in Cardfile is updated.

Start by making sure the text or graphic you want to paste is in the
Clipboard.

1. Pull down the Edit menu (Alt-E), and select Picture (E).

2. Place the cursor at the point on the card where you wish
the pasted material to appear.

3. Pull down Cardfile's Edit (Alt-E) menu and select Paste
Link (L).

PRINTING A CARD FILE

Printing a card file is much like printing from any other Windows
program. You can either print a single card, or print all the cards in
a file. Follow the instructions below:

1. If you are printing a single card, place the card you wish
to print at the front of the file by clicking on its index line,
or press PgDn repeatedly until the card is at the front.

2. Pull down the File menu (Alt-F) and select Print (P) if you
are printing a single card, Print All (A) if you are printing
all of the cards.

SAVING A CARD FILE

Cardfile saves cards in a disk file so you can use the cards at a later time. The files are saved in a format only Cardfile can read. They are stored in the Windows directory unless you specify otherwise.

1. Pull down the File menu (Alt-F) and select Save (S). If the card file has been previously saved, you can stop here. If the file has not been saved previously, the Save As dialog box will appear, prompting you for the name of the card file.

2. Type the desired name, leaving off the file extension. Cardfile will automatically add a .CRD extension.

3. Click on OK or press ↵.

CHARACTER MAP
OPERATIONS

The Character Map utility is a Windows 3.1 application whose icon appears in the Accessories program group. Use it to insert special characters (those not directly available on a keyboard) into a document in any Windows application that works with the Clipboard. Character Map displays a grid of all the characters in the current font (or any installed Windows font you select from a list box); you select the character and paste it via the Clipboard into your Windows application. Anyone who has used the old method of painstakingly looking up ASCII codes and entering them into a document will appreciate the convenience of this feature.

For all practical purposes, you can copy as many characters as you like—it would take you hours of pointing and clicking in the Character Map utility to fill up the Clipboard. However, the characters you choose to copy into the Clipboard must be from the same font; you cannot place characters from different fonts side by side in the Characters To Copy text box.

To copy Character Map text into an application, follow these instructions:

1. Open the Accessories program group.

2. Double-click on the Character Map icon. The Character
    Map screen, shown in Figure II.5, will appear.

3. If the character you want is not displayed in the current
    font, select the Font drop-down list box by clicking on it or
    by pressing Tab until it is highlighted. Pull down the font
    list by clicking on the down arrow or pressing Alt-↓. A list
    of available fonts will appear.

4. To select the font from which you wish to copy a character,
    double-click on the font name or highlight it using the ↑ or
    ↓ key, then remove the font list by pressing Alt-↑. The grid
    will change to reflect your selection.

5. Click and hold on the character you want to copy, or press
    Tab repeatedly until the grid is selected and then use the
    direction keys to select the character. The selected charac-
    ter will be magnified on the screen.

6. Double-click on the character or press Alt-Spacebar. The
    character will appear in the Characters To Copy text box
    in the upper-right corner of the window.

7. Repeat step 6 to add another copy of the character to the
    Characters To Copy text box, or repeat steps 5–6 to add dif-
    ferent characters. The Characters text box may be too nar-
    row to display all the selected characters, but they will
    appear in the Clipboard when you copy them.

Figure II.5: The Character Map screen

8. Click on the Copy command button or press Alt-C to place the contents of the Characters To Copy text box in the Clipboard. You can click Close, or press Tab until Close is selected and then press ↵, to close the Character Map window. The selected characters will remain in the Clipboard until the Clipboard contents are replaced.

9. Paste the characters into your target application.

CLIPBOARD OPERATIONS

Windows provides a temporary storage location for graphic or textual data, called Clipboard. You can transfer data from almost any program into the Clipboard and then copy that data into a different program.

Data is copied to and from the Clipboard using the Cut, Copy, Paste, or Paste Link menu options in the Edit menu. Almost every Windows program has an Edit menu. Those programs that don't have one, such as Windows Clock, are so simple that they don't need access to the Clipboard.

You can also cut or paste data from DOS applications into the Clipboard. If the DOS program is running in full-screen mode, you must copy the full screen into the Clipboard. Also, you can paste textual data into non-windowed applications, but not graphic data.

Data in the Clipboard can be viewed, deleted, saved, and retrieved using the Clipboard Viewer.

CHANGING THE DATA DISPLAY FORMAT

Clipboard can display data in a variety of formats. Depending on whether you currently have text or a graphic in the Clipboard, the Clipboard Display menu may contain the following:

*   Auto
*   Owner display

- Text
- OEM Text
- Rich Text Format
- Bitmap
- Picture
- Link
- Palette
- Native
- Objectlink
- Ownerlink

These are described under "Options," below. To choose a format option, follow these steps:

1. Call up the Clipboard Viewer.

2. Pull down the Display (Alt-D) menu.

3. Select the Display format you wish. (See "Options," below.)

Options

Auto—displays the text or graphic data in its original format, after you have viewed it in a different format.

Owner display—displays the text or graphic data just as it appears in the program that generated it. The source program must be a Windows program and it must still be active, as either a window or an icon, for Owner Display to be available. If the originating program is not active, Owner Display will not appear as a menu option. If the image is a bit map (see below), Owner Display will not appear as an option. (That's because there would be no difference between the Owner Display image and a bit map image.)

Text—shows textual data using the default Windows system font.

Rich Text Format—preserves a text file's special formatting characteristics, such as boldfacing, italics, indenting, margins, etc., when both the source and the target programs support it. RTF is meant to be a *lingua franca* for word processors, a format that each package can read and write as well as its own, making transferring documents between different word processing programs easier.

OEM Text—turns all fonts into a nonproportionally spaced (monospaced) courier font. OEM Text mode will display IBM extended characters as standard text. Data pasted from a DOS program running in full-screen mode will probably be displayed in the way it originally appeared.

Bitmap—stores graphic data as a series of colored dots. Each dot corresponds to a picture element (pixel) on the display. Bit maps are formatted according to the resolution of the display on which they are created, and for that reason are of limited usefulness. Sizing or scaling a bit map upward (making it larger) changes its appearance for the worse because the lines and angles take on a jagged appearance. The Windows Paintbrush program generates bit map files.

Picture—stores graphic images in the form of the drawing commands used by the Windows Graphic Device Interface (GDI). Because a picture is stored as GDI commands, it is not dependent on the type of display in use, and can be sized or scaled easily.

Palette—displays a color palette.

COPYING OR
CUTTING DATA INTO THE CLIPBOARD

Before you can cut or copy data, you must select it by telling the application program with which you are working what program information you want placed in the Clipboard. This is done differently in different programs. Consult the Help text file for the program you are using to learn how to select data for that program.

The following instructions apply generally to most Windows programs. Certain programs may access the Clipboard in a different way.

- With the data you wish to cut or copy selected, pull down the Edit menu (Alt-E) and select Cut (T) or Copy (C), or press Ctrl-X to cut or Ctrl-C to copy. (If you are working with version 3.0, press Shift-Del to cut or Shift-Ins to copy.)

Cut copies the selected data into the Clipboard and deletes it from whatever program you are using. Copy will not delete the data.

Some programs that support object linking and embedding (OLE) may have additional menu options that allow you to cut or copy only and do not implement any OLE connections. This means that when you paste this data into another application there will be no link back to the source application.

Copying Data from a Windowed DOS Program

A windowed DOS program is a standard MS-DOS program that appears inside a window. Windows will run windowed DOS programs only when it is operating in 386 Enhanced mode. The window used for windowed DOS programs does not have a menu bar. It has only one menu—the Control menu—and all copying and pasting is done from there. You cannot cut data from a non-windowed DOS application.

The Control menu option that allows you to cut and paste from DOS programs is called Edit. Selecting Edit brings up a cascading menu that has Mark, Copy, Paste, and Scroll options; this menu is shown in Figure II.6.

1. With the windowed DOS program on the screen, pull down the Control menu by clicking on the Control menu button or by pressing Alt-Spacebar, select Edit (E), and then select Mark (K). Place the mouse pointer at the upper-left corner of the on-screen information you wish to copy. Click and hold down the left mouse button and drag the mouse pointer to the lower-right corner of the information to be copied.

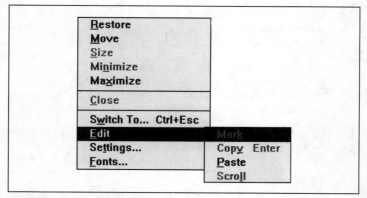

Figure II.6: The open Edit menu with cascade

2.   Release the mouse button.

3.   Pull down the Control menu and select Edit (E).

4.   Select Copy (Y).

Copying Data from a
Non-Windowed DOS Program

A non-windowed DOS program is a standard MS-DOS program
that runs under Windows, but takes up the entire screen. In Windows parlance, the program is running in "full-screen mode." Out-
wardly, it looks like a standard DOS application and there is no
evidence that Windows is present at all. To switch back to Windows, you press special key sequences (Alt-Tab or Alt-Esc).

You can copy data from one of these full-screen DOS programs, but
you must copy the entire screen. You cannot cut data from a non-windowed DOS program; you can only copy it. Also, because the Windows mouse pointer is unavailable when a DOS program is operating
in full-screen mode, all copying is done using key sequences.

•   With the DOS program you wish to work with on the
    screen, press PrtSc (on newer keyboards, this key may be
    labeled *Print Screen*). If this command doesn't work, it
    may be because you have an older keyboard. Try Alt-PrtSc
    or Shift-PrtSc.

Notes   Normally you can't copy graphics from full-screen DOS
programs running under Windows: you can copy only text.

Copying Windows Screens into the Clipboard

Windows comes with a built-in screen-capture facility. You can, at any
time, press a key sequence and capture the entire current Windows
desktop in the Clipboard. You can press a different key sequence
and capture only the currently active window.

The data captured in this way is stored in the form of a bit map. It
can be pasted into Windows Paintbrush workspace and edited,
then saved as a Windows bit map (.BMP extension) or as a PC

Paintbrush file (.PCX extension). The latter file format is understood by a wide variety of programs.

1. Position the windows you wish to capture. Size and move them until you are satisfied with the way they look.

2. Press PrtSc and the entire Windows desktop—open windows, icons, everything—will be copied into the Clipboard. Press Alt-PrtSc if you want only the currently active window to be copied into the Clipboard.

Notes The Windows screen-capture facility is useful, but it has some pitfalls. You cannot, for example, use the Alt-PrtSc combination to capture the image of a window with a menu pulled down. The moment you touch the Alt key, Windows assumes you are going to pull down a different menu, and closes the one that is currently on-screen. You have to capture the entire desktop to get an image of a pulled-down menu.

DELETING CLIPBOARD DATA

Once you have finished using the Clipboard to move data between programs, it is a good idea to delete that data from the Clipboard. This frees up memory that Windows can use. To remove the data from the Clipboard, follow these instructions:

1. Call up the Clipboard Viewer and pull down the Edit menu (Alt-E).

2. Select Delete (D). A dialog box will appear, asking you to confirm the deletion.

3. Select Yes or press ⏎.

Notes If you have data stored in the Clipboard you think you may need, you can save it in a file and load it back into the Clipboard later. See "Saving Clipboard's Contents" and "Retrieving Clipboard's Contents."

PASTING DATA FROM THE CLIPBOARD

To paste data from the Clipboard is to copy material that has been stored temporarily in the Clipboard into a program. You can paste textual or graphic data into any program that supports the type of data being transferred.

The following instructions apply generally to most Windows programs. Certain programs may access the Clipboard in a different way.

- Call up the Clipboard Viewer to make sure the data you wish to paste is in the Clipboard. (See "Viewing the Clipboard.") Pull down the Edit menu (E) and select Paste (P), or press Ctrl-V. (If you are working with version 3.0, press Shift-Ins instead.)

Notes   When you paste data into a Windows program, the data is not deleted from the Clipboard. There are only two ways to delete data from the Clipboard: use the Clipboard Viewer to delete it (see "Deleting Clipboard Data"), or overwrite it by cutting or copying new data into the Clipboard.

Establishing a Paste Link Using the Clipboard

Using Windows' object linking and embedding (OLE) technology, you can define a link between a data file you are currently working on and another that is stored on disk and/or is being used by a different program. For example, you can display a graphic image with Paintbrush, copy that image into the Clipboard, call up another program such as Write, paste link the image from the Clipboard into the Write document (or data file), and then save the document file. Then, whenever you edit the image in the Write document file, the Paintbrush file will be opened and you will be able to save your edits in the original Paintbrush file.

The following instructions apply generally to most Windows programs. Certain programs may implement Paste Link in a different way. Note that both programs, the target and the source, must support OLE.

1. Make sure the data you wish to paste is in the Clipboard. (See "Copying or Cutting Data into the Clipboard.")

2. In your application, position the cursor at the point where you want the linked material to appear.

3. Pull down the Edit menu (Alt-E).

4. Select Paste Link (L).

Pasting Data into a Windowed DOS Program

Pasting data into a windowed DOS program is very similar to pasting data into a Windows program, with one notable exception: you can paste only unformatted textual data into a DOS program.

1.   Make sure the data you wish to paste is in the Clipboard. (See "Viewing the Clipboard.")

2.   In the DOS program, position the cursor at the point where you wish to paste the text.

3.   Pull down the Control menu (Alt-Spacebar).

4.   Select Edit (E). A cascaded submenu will appear.

5.   From the cascaded submenu, select Paste (P).

Pasting Data into a Non-Windowed DOS Program

Windows has no facility for allowing you to paste text into a non-windowed DOS application while it is on-screen. Instead, you must shrink the full-screen DOS program to an icon and then select the Paste option from its Control menu. Follow these steps:

1.   Make sure the data you wish to paste is in the Clipboard. (See "Viewing the Clipboard.")

2.   In the DOS program into which you are going to paste data, position the cursor *exactly* at the point where you want the pasted text to appear.

3.   Press Alt-Esc to switch back to the Windows desktop. The non-windowed DOS application will be reduced to an icon, which appears at the bottom of the desktop screen.

4.   Click once on the DOS program's icon. Or, Press Alt-Esc repeatedly until the icon is selected, then press Alt-Spacebar to pull down the program's Control menu.

6.   Select Edit (E). A cascaded submenu will appear.

7.   From the cascaded submenu, select Paste (P). Windows will copy text out of the Clipboard and into the DOS application. From the application's perspective, it will be just as if the text were typed at the keyboard.

8. Maximize the DOS program icon by double-clicking on it. If you are using a keyboard, select the icon, press Alt-Spacebar to pull down the Control menu, and select Restore (R).

Notes You may find that Windows is not particularly good at pasting data into non-windowed DOS applications. Make sure that you check the results of each paste operation thoroughly.

RETRIEVING THE CLIPBOARD'S CONTENTS

Data that appears in the Clipboard can be stored in Clipboard files, which by default have a .CLP extension (see "Saving Clipboard's Contents"). When the time comes to use data that has been saved in a file, you can use the Clipboard Viewer to retrieve the file.

1. Call up the Clipboard Viewer, pull down the File menu (Alt-F), and select Open (O). A dialog box that lists all the Clipboard files in the current directory will appear.

2. If the Clipboard currently contains data, a message box appears, asking if the contents of the Clipboard should be cleared. Select Yes.

3. Double-click on the name of the Clipboard file you wish to retrieve, or highlight the file name and then select OK or press ⏎.

Notes The Clipboard Viewer will retrieve only .CLP files.

SAVING THE CLIPBOARD'S CONTENTS

Because the Clipboard is often used to transfer important data, you may wish to save the Clipboard's contents as a file. By default, Clipboard files have a .CLP extension.

1. Call up the Clipboard Viewer, pull down the File menu (Alt-F), and select Save As (A). A dialog box that lists all the Clipboard files in the current directory will appear. The File Name text box contains the default file extension, *.CLP.

2.   In the File Name text box, type in a name for the Clip-
     board file. The .CLP extension will be added automat-
     ically, unless you specify another extension.

3.   Select OK or press ⏎.

Notes   Clipboard files are unrelated to the .CLP files used by the
Quattro Pro spreadsheet program; the file types are not compatible.

UNDOING A CUT OR PASTE

Once you have cut or pasted data to or from a Windows program,
you may see that you have made a mistake. Most Windows
programs offer you an Undo option, which will delete the most current Cut or Paste command and return the workspace to the state it
was in before the command was executed. Some standard DOS
programs offer their own form of Undo, but the procedures
described below are for Windows programs only.

These instructions assume that you have just cut or pasted a text or
graphic, and that you wish to undo what you have done. They
apply generally to most Windows programs.

*   Pull down the Edit menu and select Undo, or press Ctrl-Z
    (if you are using version 3.0, press Alt-Backspace). The
    window's workspace will revert to the way it was before
    you executed the Cut or Paste command.

VIEWING THE CLIPBOARD

You can view the contents of the Clipboard at any time by calling
up the Clipboard Viewer. You can also use the Clipboard Viewer to
delete the contents of the Clipboard, change the format in which
data is displayed by the Clipboard Viewer, save the Clipboard's
contents to a file, or retrieve a file containing Clipboard data.

1.   Cut or copy some data into the Clipboard. (See "Copying
     or Cutting Data into the Clipboard.")

2.   With the Main group window active, double-click on the
     Clipboard icon or use the direction keys to highlight it and
     press ⏎. Whatever data is in the Clipboard will be visible
     immediately in the Clipboard Viewer's window.

THE CLOCK UTILITY

Another accessory program included with Windows is Clock, which provides an on-screen analog or digital clock. When minimized to an icon, Clock continues to keep the correct time and displays it in the icon. Since Clock uses only about 12K of memory, you can keep a timepiece on your Windows desktop just as you would on your real desktop.

To display the clock, follow these steps:

1. Open the Accessories program group.

2. Double-click on the Clock icon, or move to the icon using the direction keys and press ↵. The Clock window appears in whatever mode it was in last. The default mode is Analog.

Options To set Clock options, see "Changing to Analog or Digital Clock," and "Removing the Title Bar of the Clock Window." Other Clock options available are:

- From the Settings pull-down menu:

  Seconds (S)—displayed in both the Analog and Digital clock windows.

  Date (D)—displayed on the title bar of the Analog clock, in the Digital clock's window, or in the icon description of the minimized clock.

- From the Clock's Control menu:

  Always on Top—keeps the Clock or Clock icon visible on the desktop. To select or deselect Always on Top, with the Clock selected, click on the Control menu button and click on Always on Top, or press Alt-Spacebar to pull down the Control menu and press T.

CHANGING TO ANALOG OR DIGITAL CLOCK

The analog display is circular and has hour, minute, and second sweep hands. The digital display shows the current time in hours, minutes, and seconds in the format *HH:MM:SS*.

- Pull down the Settings (Alt-S) menu and select Analog (A) or Digital (D).

REMOVING THE TITLE BAR OF THE CLOCK WINDOW

When you display the Clock on your desktop, you may find it distracting to see the Clock title bar along with any other open applications on your desktop. You can remove the Clock window's title bar by pulling down the Settings menu and clicking on No Title (N). Only the time will appear in the Clock window. (The date will appear in the Digital clock window if selected as an option.) To restore the Clock's title bar, double-click in the Clock window, or select the window (press Alt-Esc until the Clock window is the top window on the desktop) and press Esc.

CONFIGURING WINDOWS WITH THE CONTROL PANEL

The Control Panel is a utility program that lets you configure Windows in many ways. You can change the default printer and printer port, install a new printer driver, install new fonts, customize the mouse, or change the time and date. You can also do some fun things, like permanently change the colors that Windows uses, or use a graphic image generated in Paintbrush as a backdrop for the Windows desktop. All of the above procedures are described in the following pages.

The Control Panel is a Windows program, so naturally it has a program icon. The Control Panel program icon looks like a desktop computer with a mouse attached and a clock to the left. It is located in the Main program group. While you run the Control Panel just as you would any other Windows program (see "Running an Application Program"), the Control Panel is unlike most other Windows programs. Its workspace doesn't contain a blank area for graphics or text. Rather, it contains a number of icons that represent options within the Control Panel; see Figure II.7.

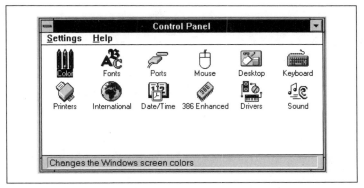

Figure II.7: The Control Panel window

If you are not running Windows in 386 Enhanced Mode, the 386 Enhanced mode icon does not appear. Similarly, if you are not on a network, Windows does not display the network icon.

Each Control Panel option, when invoked, produces a window of some kind. Unlike the document windows produced by other programs, the windows generated by the Control Panel are closed with the standard key sequence for closing an application window (Alt-F4), not the key sequence that closes program group windows (Ctrl-F4).

There are two ways to invoke a Control Panel option:

1. Open the Control Panel window.

2. Click on the icon of the option you wish to invoke, or press Alt-S to pull down the Settings menu and use the direction keys to select the menu option.

3. Click the mouse twice in rapid succession or press ↵.

CHANGING WINDOWS' COLOR SCHEME

A *color scheme* is the series of colors assigned to the component parts—borders, title bars, etc.—of the Windows environment. After installation, Windows comes up in a default color scheme composed of grays, whites, and blues. Included with Windows are 22 other color schemes. You can switch to any of these schemes using the Control Panel.

1. Run the Color option. A dialog box will appear, with the Color Schemes drop-down list box in the upper portion.

2. Click on the down arrow at the right edge of the drop-down list box, or press Alt-↓. A list of alternate color schemes will appear.

3. Click on the scheme of your choice, or use the direction keys to highlight the name of the color scheme. The lower portion of the dialog box will display the new color scheme.

4. Click on OK or press ↵.

Modifying a Color Scheme

You aren't limited to the color schemes in the list. You can modify the current scheme and assign any color to any component of the Windows interface. Once you've modified the current color scheme, you can save it under a new name. (See "Saving a Color Scheme.")

1. Run the Color option. (See the instructions under "Configuring Windows with the Control Panel.")

2. Click on the Color Palette command button (Alt-P).

3. Click on the down arrow in the Screen Element drop-down list box or press Alt-↓ to pull down the list. Click on the element you wish to change (use the scroll arrows if necessary) or use the direction keys to highlight the name of the element and press Alt-↑.

4. Select a color for that element by clicking on your choice in the Basic Colors palette; or press Tab, use the direction keys to choose the color, and press Spacebar to

selectit. Your changes will be displayed on the left side of the Color dialog box.

5.   Repeat steps 3–4 for every element you wish to change.

6.   If desired, save the color scheme for future use. (See "Saving a Color Scheme.")

7.   Click on OK or press ↵. The Color dialog box will close and Windows will adopt the modified color scheme.

Removing a Color Scheme

You can remove any color schemes you create, or any of the color schemes that come with Windows (except Windows Default).

1.   Run the Color option.

2.   Select the color scheme you wish to remove. (See the instructions under "Changing Windows' Color Scheme.")

3.   To delete the current color scheme, click on Remove Scheme (Alt-M). A message box will appear, asking you to confirm the removal.

4.   Click on Yes or press ↵. If you wish, you may then click Cancel, or press Tab repeatedly until Cancel is highlighted and press ↵. This will close the Color dialog box, retaining your selected color scheme. (If you click OK, you may be choosing a new color scheme.)

Saving a Color Scheme

You can save a color scheme and assign it a name, which will then appear in the Color Schemes drop-down list box. The Control Panel will not allow you save an existing color scheme—you must first modify a color scheme before saving it. (See "Modifying a Color Scheme.")

1.   Click on Save Scheme (Alt-A). A dialog box will appear, prompting you to name the modified scheme.

2.   Accept the current name or type a new name, then click on OK or press ↵.

DATE AND TIME

Windows uses your computer's internal clock to keep track of the
date and time. You can use the Control Panel to change the date and
time settings.

1. Run the Date/Time option. The Date & Time dialog box
will appear. There will be two miniature scroll boxes in it,
labeled Date (Alt-D) and labeled Time (Alt-T).

2. The highlight appears on the month value in the Date
area. Select the value you wish to change by clicking on
month, day, or year; in the Time area, you can click on
hours, minutes, or seconds. To make your selection using
the keyboard, press Tab to move the highlight forward
through the Date and Time values or Shift-Tab to move
backward.

3. Click on the scroll arrows or use the direction keys to
change the highlighted value, or you can key in the value
directly.

4. Click on OK or press ↵.

Notes   When Windows changes the time and date, it not only
modifies the software clock maintained by MS-DOS; it also changes
the time and date in the battery-run CMOS RAM clock on your
computer's main board. This means that the correct time and date
are maintained even when the computer is turned off. It also means
that you don't have to use a CMOS RAM setup program to change
settings in your computer's clock; you can use Windows.

THE DESKTOP DISPLAY

The components of the Windows desktop display you can configure include the desktop pattern, the desktop wallpaper, the
screen saver, the sizing grid, and the cursor blink rate. The color
scheme, which can also be changed, is controlled by the Color icon
under the Control Panel; see "Changing Windows' Color Scheme."

Changing the Desktop Pattern

Windows offers you the ability to overlay the Windows desktop with a graphic pattern. The Control Panel has several stored patterns, along with an editor that lets you create custom patterns.

1. Run the Desktop option. A dialog box will appear, with the Names drop-down list box displayed in Pattern area in the upper portion of the box.

2. Click on the down arrow at the right edge of the Names drop-down list box. A list of patterns will appear.

3. Click on the pattern of your choice, or use the direction keys to highlight the pattern.

4. Click on OK or press ↵.

Notes   If you have both a desktop pattern and a wallpaper graphic active (see "Changing the Desktop Wallpaper"), the wallpaper will take precedence. You will see the pattern only where the wallpaper is not visible.

Changing the Desktop Wallpaper

Windows offers you the ability to change the Windows desktop from a single color to a graphic image. The images are stored in a bitmap file of the type produced by Windows Paintbrush. (Bitmap files have a .BMP extension). Windows has several stored bitmap files that can be used as wallpaper.

1. Run the Desktop option. A dialog box will appear, with the Wallpaper area displayed just under the center of the box.

2. Click on the down arrow at the right edge of the File drop-down list box. Or, press Tab repeatedly until the File drop-down list box is highlighted and press Alt-↓. A list of .BMP files will appear.

3. Click on the file of your choice, or use the direction keys to highlight the file name and then press Alt-↑ to remove the drop-down list.

4. Click on the Center or Tile option button, or press Alt-C (Center) or Alt-T (Tile).

Center—centers the wallpaper, both horizontally and vertically, on the Windows desktop.

Tile—duplicates the wallpaper and sets it down in a pattern on the desktop. Tile will work only if the selected bitmap is small enought to allow for tiling.

5. Click on OK or press ↵.

Notes   Windows comes with several bitmap files, but not all are useful as desktop backgrounds. One way to assemble a collection of bitmap files is to look for graphic files with a .PCX extension, which are produced by ZSoft's PC Paintbrush program. Files with the .PCX extension are common; most graphics programs either import or export .PCX files. Microsoft Paint files can also be used—they have an .MSP extension. Once you have a .PCX or .MSP file, you can use Windows Paintbrush to convert it to a .BMP file. Such files, however, cannot be changed back to their original format.

Fast Application Switching

The Fast "Alt+Tab" Switching option in the Applications area of the Desktop is a new feature in Windows 3.1. Fast "Alt+Tab" Switching allows you to cycle through the open Windows applications and activate the needed program in one step. By holding down the Alt key, pressing Tab until you reach the desired program, and then releasing both keys, the selected program is activated. If the application is minimized, releasing both keys restores it. To return to your original application, press Esc while you are still holding down the Alt key. The default setting for this option in enabled.

Icon Settings

In the Icons area of the Desktop dialog box, the spacing between icons may be reset and you may specify that the icon title text be wrapped to a second line (the default).

1. Click on the up arrow to increase or the down arrow to decrease the number of pixels between icons in the Spacing text box. Or, press Alt-S and type in the new number of pixels. The maximum space between icons is 512 pixels.

2. If desired, click on the Wrap Title check box or press Alt-W to disable the icon-title wrapping feature.

3. If you have made changes in the Icons area, you must click OK or press ↵ in the Desktop dialog box to activate them.

The Screen Saver

Screen Saver is a new feature in Windows 3.1. The Windows Screen Saver is a moving design that appears on your screen when no mouse movements or keyboard selections are made after a specified amount of time. One of its most important functions is to prevent screen burn-in. If used with a password, Screen Saver will also prevent unauthorized access to your work while you are away from your computer. When the Screen Saver has been selected, it will be automatically activated each time Windows is used.

1. With the Desktop dialog box open, click on the Name drop-down list arrow button in the Screen Saver area, or press Tab repeatedly until the Name text box is high-lighted and then press Alt-↓ to display the list of available Screen Saver patterns.

2. Click with the mouse or use the direction keys to select a name on the list. Click Test or press Alt-E to see a sample of the selected Screen Saver pattern. To return to the Desktop dialog box, click the mouse button, move the mouse, or press any key on the keyboard. Repeat this step until the desired Screen Saver pattern is selected.

3. Click the up button to increase or the down button to decrease the delay interval, or press Alt-D and type in the new delay interval.

4. Click Setup (Alt-U). The Screen Saver Setup dialog box appears, with unique options for each of the available Screen Saver patterns. Select the options you desire for the chosen Screen Saver pattern and then click OK or press ↵.

5. Click OK or press ↵ in the Desktop dialog box.

Setting a Password for the Screen Saver

It sometimes may be useful to hide the work on your screen when you are away from your computer. Setting a password will prevent unauthorized access to your work.

1. In the Screen Saver Setup dialog box, enable Password Protected by clicking on it, or press Alt-P. The Set Password button becomes available.

2. Click on Set Password (S), to display the Change Password dialog box.

3. Type in the password in the New Password (Alt-N) text box. (To ensure your privacy, Windows will display a series of asterisks in the text box, instead of the password itself.)

4. Select the Retype New Password (Alt-R) text box and type the password again, exactly as you did in step 3.

5. Click OK or press ↵ to confirm the password.

If you wish to change an old password, follow these steps:

1. Click on Set Password (S).

2. Type the current password in the Old Password text box.

3. Repeat steps 3–5 above.

When password protection is enabled and the selected Screen Saver pattern is on-screen, your work can be recalled to the screen only by those who know your password. To remove the Screen Saver pattern and return to your work, follow these steps:

1. Move or click the mouse or press any key. A dialog box, named for the Screen Saver pattern you are currently using, appears.

2. Type your password in the Password text box.

3. Click OK or press ↵.

Notes   Password protection is not available for the Blank Screen Saver pattern. When a password has been selected, it will remain in effect for any new Screen Saver pattern you select, provided that password protection is enabled for the new pattern.

The Sizing Grid

The sizing grid is an invisible series of horizontal and vertical lines with which icons and windows will align themselves, if you so specify. When the sizing grid is inactive, you can place icons anywhere you like on the screen; this can result in a confusing overlapping of icons, or scattered icons. When the sizing grid is active, icons will "snap" to (move to and line up with) the nearest grid line. The Sizing Grid dialog box allows you to set the granularity of the grid and the border width of all windows on the desktop.

1. Run the Desktop option. A dialog box will appear, displaying the Sizing Grid box in the lower-left corner. It shows two scroll boxes, Granularity and Border Width.

2. To adjust the size of the grid, click on the arrows of the Granularity scroll box to scroll the numbers up or down. Or, select Gruanularity and type the number in the text box. The grid expands by 8 pixels each time you increase the value by 1. The maximum number is 49 and the minimum is 0. A value of 0 turns the grid off. Or, to adjust the width of window borders, click on the arrows of the Border Width scroll box to scroll the numbers up or down. Or, select Border Width (Alt-B) and type the number in the text box. The border expands by 1 pixel each time you increase the value by 1. The maximum number is 50 and the minimum is 1.

3. Click on OK.

DEVICE DRIVERS

The Drivers option in the Control Panel allows you to add, remove, or reconfigure drivers for devices such as sound or video equipment. Windows cannot recognize these devices until the appropriate drivers are correctly installed and configured. The Drivers component of the Control Panel is new in Windows 3.1.

Adding a New Driver

1. Activate the Drivers option. The Drivers dialog box will
    appear with a list of currently installed drivers. Click Add
    (Alt-A).

2. Double-click on the name of the driver you wish to install,
    or highlight the name using the direction keys and press
    ↵. The Install Driver dialog box will appear.

3. Type the letter of the drive containing the Windows dis-
    kette indicated or accept the default drive letter by click-
    ing OK or pressing ↵. Change diskettes as requested by
    the dialog box.

4. When the new driver is installed, a message box will appear
    to inform you that Windows must be restarted for the new
    driver to be used. If you wish to add another driver, click
    Don't Restart Now or press ↵. If you are ready to use the
    newly installed driver, click Restart Now or press Alt-R.

5. When all required drivers have been installed, click Close
    or press Tab repeatedly until Close is highlighted to
    remove the Drivers dialog box.

Removing a Driver

1. Activate the Drivers option.

2. Highlight the name of the driver you wish to remove from
    the Installed Drivers list.

3. Click Remove or press Alt-R. A message box will
    appear requesting confirmation of the removal.
    Click Yes or press ↵.

4. The System Setting Change message box appears, inform-
    ing you that the removal will not occur until you have re-
    started Windows. Click Don't Restart Now or press ↵, or
    click Restart Now (Alt-R).

5. Click Close or press Tab repeatedly until Close is high-
    lighted to remove the Drivers dialog box.

Setting Up a Driver

Some drivers call for additional information in order to work with Windows. If a selected driver does not need more or different information, the Setup button is dimmed.

1. With the Drivers window open, highlight the name of the driver you want to add or for which you want to change setup information.

2. Click on Setup or press Alt-S. The setup information required for that driver will appear. Make changes as necessary.

3. Click OK or press ↵.

4. Click Close or press Tab repeatedly until Close is highlighted to remove the Drivers dialog box.

INTERNATIONAL SETTINGS

The International option in the Control Panel allows you to reconfigure settings such as date and time. In this way, Windows may be customized to change the International settings for applications that require a different format.

The basic settings include country, language, keyboard layout, measurement, and list separator. If you select a country, the other basic settings will change to reflect the options for that country. Any of these settings may be customized as desired.

1. Activate the International option on the Control Panel. The International dialog box will appear.

2. To select the Country (Alt-C), Language (Alt-L), Keyboard Layout (Alt-K), or Measurement (Alt-M) item, click on the drop-down list arrow, or use the key sequence for the item you want to change and press Alt-↓ to reveal the list of available choices.

3. Click on your choice in the selected item's list, or use the direction keys to highlight your choice and then press Alt-↑. Change as many of these items as necessary to customize the settings.

4. Change the List Separator by pressing Tab repeatedly until the cursor is in the text box or highlight the text box by pressing Alt-S. Type in the new list separator.

5. Click OK or press ↵.

Changing the International Date Format

Some Windows applications use a date function. The date format selected in International settings will be used by these applications.

1. Activate the International option on the Control Panel. The International dialog box will appear.

2. In the International dialog box, click Change in the Date Format area, or press Alt-D. The International-Date Format dialog box will open.

3. In the Short Date Format area, select the Order (Alt-O) for the display of day-month-year values by clicking on the option button or by using the direction keys to select the option.

4. Select Separator (Alt-S) and type in the desired month-day-year separator.

5. Enable (or disable) the Day Leading Zero (Alt-D), Month Leading Zero (Alt-M) and/or the Century (Alt-C) options by clicking on their check boxes or using the key sequences. (See "Options," below.)

6. To change the month-day-year order in the Long Date Format, select the Order (Alt-R) for the display of day-month-year values by clicking on the option button or by using the direction keys to select the option.

7. Change the display of day of the week, month, day value, and year by clicking on the arrow button, or press Tab to highlight the item to change and press Alt-↓. The item's drop-down list will appear. Select one of the available options by clicking on it or by using the direction keys and then pressing Alt-↑. (See "Options," below.)

8. Change the displayed date separators by pressing Tab repeatedly until the text box is highlighted. Then type in the new separator.

9. Each change you make in the Long Date Format area appears in the sample date at the bottom of the area. When your date is displayed as you wish, click OK or press ⌐.

10. In the International dialog box, click OK or press Tab repeatedly until OK is highlighted and press ⌐.

Options

Day display— displayed as a whole word or an abbreviation.

Month display— displayed as a whole word or an abbreviation.

Day of the month—day values less than 10 can be displayed with or without a leading zero.

Century— displayed as two- or four-digit numbers.

Changing the International Time Format

The time can be configured in a 12- or 24-hour format. Suffixes can be added to the time, and you can choose to have leading zeros for the single-digit hours.

1. Activate the International option on the Control Panel. The International dialog box will appear.

2. In the International dialog box, click Change in the Time Format area or press Alt-T. The International-Time Format dialog box appears.

3. Click 12 Hour (Alt-2) or 24 Hour (Alt-4) to select either time format option, or use the direction keys.

4. Click in the text box or press Tab to move the cursor to the text box if you wish to add a suffix. Type in the suffix. If you are adding a second suffix (i.e., AM and PM), select the next text box and type in the second suffix. Only one suffix may be added if the 24-hour format is selected.

5. If you wish to change the separator, press Tab to reach the Separator text box or press Alt-S. Type in the new separator.

6. Click on the option button or press Alt-L and use the direction keys to select or deselect leading zeros.

7. Click OK or press ↵ to accept the new time format.

8. In the International dialog box, click OK or press Tab repeatedly until OK is highlighted and press ↵.

Changing the International Currency Format

The Currency Format can be changed to reflect currencies in different countries. The currency symbol and its placement, negative value formats, and the number of places displayed after the decimal point can be changed.

1. Activate the International option on the Control Panel. The International dialog box will appear.

2. In the International dialog box, click on Change in the Currency Format area or press Alt-U. The International-Currency Format dialog box appears.

3. Click on the arrow button or press Alt-P and then press Alt-↓ to open the Symbol Placement drop-down list. Click on the symbol placement format, or use the direction keys to highlight the format example and press Alt-↑.

4. Click on the arrow button or press Alt-N and then press Alt-↓ to open the Negative drop-down list. Click on the negative format, or use the direction keys to highlight the format example and press Alt-↑.

5. Tab to the Symbol text box or press Alt-S to move it. Type in the new symbol.

6. Tab to the Decimal Digits text box or press Alt-D to move to it. Type in the new number.

7. Click OK or press ↵.

8. In the International dialog box, click OK or press Tab repeatedly until OK is highlighted and press ↵.

Changing the International Number Format

The Number Format options in International settings allows you to define the display of numbers in Windows applications.

1. Activate the International option on the Control Panel. The International dialog box will appear.

2. In the International dialog box, click on Change in the Number Format area or press Alt-N. The International-Number Format dialog box appears.

3. Use the Tab key to highlight the 1000 Separator (Alt-S), Decimal Separator (Alt-D), or Decimal Digits (Alt-E) text box. Type in the punctuation or digit. (See "Options," below.)

4. Click on the Leading Zero option button or press Alt-L and use the direction keys to choose whether numbers smaller than 1 will display a leading zero.

5. Click OK or press ↵.

Options

1000 Separator—the comma or other punctuation used to group digits in thousands.

Decimal Separator—the period or other punctuation used to separate whole numbers from the fractional portion of a decimal number.

Decimal Digits—the number of places to appear in a decimal number after the selected separator.

Notes   The defaults in the International options of Control Panel are standard United States English settings.

THE MOUSE

You can adjust the following aspects of the mouse's operations in Windows: the double-click speed, the tracking speed, Mouse Trails mode (for laptop computers), and the primary button designation.

Adjusting the Double-Click Speed

The double-click speed is the period of time allowed between the two clicks that constitute a double click. If the double-click rate is fast, you must click very quickly for Windows to recogize the double click. If the double-click rate is slow, you can click at a more deliberate pace.

1. Run the Mouse option. The Mouse dialog box will appear.

2. Click on the Double-Click Speed scroll bar to change the double-click rate. Or, press Alt-D and use the direction keys to increase or decrease the double-click speed. The change takes effect the moment the scroll button is moved.

3. Double-click the TEST box. If the box becomes highlighted (or if an already highlighted box returns to normal video), the double click was successful.

4. Move between the Double-Click Speed scroll bar and the TEST box, adjusting and testing the double-click rate until it suits you.

5. Click on OK or press ↵ to save the adjusted rate.

Adjusting the Mouse Tracking Speed

The tracking speed is the rate at which the mouse pointer moves across the Windows screen, relative to the distance the mouse is moved across your work surface. If the tracking speed is set too slow, you must move the mouse farther on the desk to make the pointer move the desired distance across the screen. Different tracking speeds are comfortable for different people, so the Control Panel allows you to adjust the rate.

1. Run the Mouse option. The Mouse dialog box will appear.

2. Click on the Mouse Tracking Speed scroll bar to change the tracking speed. Or, use the direction keys to increase or decrease the mouse tracking speed. The change takes effect the moment you move the scroll box. If the speed is

very low, it may seem like the pointer is responding slug-
gishly to the mouse. Move the scroll box toward the Fast
setting until the mouse speed feels comfortable.

3.   Click on OK or press ↲ to save the adjustment.

Mouse Trails

Windows 3.1 offers another operating mode for the mouse, called
Mouse Trails. Select this option to leave a trail, or an after-image on
the screen, of the mouse pointer movements.

Mouse Trails is intended to help you find the mouse pointer on the
LCD screen of a laptop computer. LCD screens typically display an
indistinct mouse pointer—the trail left when this option is enabled
allows you to use the mouse pointer more easily.

1.   Run the Mouse option. The Mouse dialog box will appear.

2.   Select the Mouse Trails check box.

3.   Click on OK or press ↲.

Swapping Mouse Buttons

Under Windows, the left mouse button is designated the primary
mouse button. This enables a right-handed person to easily move
the mouse and click with his or her right index finger. Left-handed
people often find this arrangement bothersome, so Windows lets
you make the right mouse button the primary button.

1.   Run the Mouse option. The Mouse dialog box will appear.

2.   Click on the Swap Left/Right Mouse Buttons check box.
The mouse button switches immediately.

3.   Using the newly designated mouse button, click
on OK.

PRINTERS AND FONTS

Installing a Font

Windows considers a font to be a graphically rendered image of a particular typeface. Fonts are named after the typefaces they represent—Courier, Times Roman, Helvetica, etc. Windows is able to display fonts on-screen and print them using data stored in a font file. A font can represent a particular type size, or it can be "scalable."

Windows is shipped with fonts adequate for most tasks, but certain users of Windows will find that they need additional fonts. The Control Panel allows you to add font files, and therefore fonts, to the Windows environment.

When you are adding a font, you must have a disk with the new font files on it, or the new files must be somewhere on your hard disk.

1.   Run the Fonts option. The Fonts dialog box will appear.

2.   Click on the Add command button (Alt-A). The Add Fonts dialog box will appear.

3.   If necessary, place the disk containing the new font files in the floppy-disk drive.

4.   To select the new drive, click on the arrow button in the Drives list box, or press Alt-V and then Alt-↓ to reveal the list. Click on the drive or use the direction keys to highlight it. To select a new directory, make sure the correct drive is displayed in the Drives list box. Then, in the Directories list box, double-click on the desired directory (usually the parent directory, i.e., C:\) or press Alt-D, use the direction keys to highlight the directory and press ↵. Click on the scroll button and drag it until the name of the desired directory is displayed, then double-click on the directory name. Or, use the direction keys to highlight the directory name and press ↵. Once the appropriate disk or directory is selected, the names of the fonts will appear in the List of Fonts list box.

5.   Click on the name of the font file you wish to add in the List of Fonts list box. To select multiple fonts, hold the Ctrl key down and click on each one. Or, press Alt-F and use

the direction keys to highlight the name of the font file and press ⏎. To select multiple fonts, hold the Shift key down as you press the direction key.

6. If you want to save space on your disk, disable the Copy Fonts to Windows Directory (Alt-C) option by clicking on it. Windows will access the files in their current drive and directory. If the Copy Fonts to Windows Directory option is enabled, the selected fonts will be placed in the System subdirectory of Windows.

7. Click on OK.

8. When the Fonts dialog box reappears, click on Cancel. Or, press Tab repeatedly until Cancel is selected, then press ⏎.

Installing a New Printer

If you change printers, or get an additional printer, you will need to prepare Windows to access and use your new device. This involves using the Control Panel to "tell" Windows about the new printer and to copy a special configuration file, called a *printer driver,* onto your hard disk. You will need your original Windows installation disks for this procedure.

1. Run the Printers option. The Printers dialog box will appear.

2. Click on the Add (Alt-A) command button. The dialog box will expand until it appears similar to the one in Figure II.8.

3. Scroll through the List of Printers until the name of your printer appears. Click on the name or use the direction keys to highlight it.

4. Click on Install (Alt-I). A dialog box will appear, asking you to insert a specific Windows installation disk in the floppy-disk drive.

5. Insert the disk in the floppy-disk drive, then click on OK or press ⏎.

Notes   If the name of your printer does not appear on the list, Windows does not have a driver for that printer. Check your

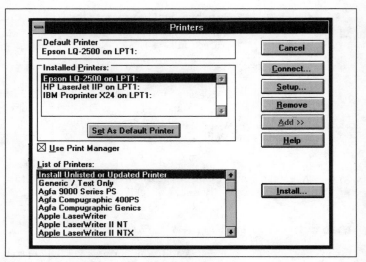

Figure II.8: The Printers dialog box with list box

printer's manual to see if the printer is supported by another printer driver that does appear on the list.

Removing a Font

The Control Panel allows you to remove fonts from the Windows environment. You may want to do this if your fonts are taking up too much hard-disk space.

1. Run the Fonts option. The Fonts dialog box will appear.

2. Scroll through the Installed Fonts list box to find the name of the desired font. Click on the name or use the direction keys to highlight it.

3. Click on the Remove (Alt-R) command button. The Remove Font dialog box will appear, asking you to confirm the font deletion. If you want not only to delete the font from Windows, but also to delete the font file itself from the hard disk, click on the Delete Font File (Alt-D) check box.

4. Click on Yes or press ⏎.

5. When the Fonts dialog box reappears, click on Close or press Tab repeatedly until Close is highlighted, then press ⏎.

Removing an Installed Printer

If you no longer need a printer, you can remove it from the list of installed printers.

1. Run the Printers option. The Printers dialog box will appear.

2. In the Installed Printers list, click on the name of the printer you wish to remove (use the scroll arrows if necessary). Or, use the direction keys to highlight its name.

3. Click Remove (Alt-R). A message box will appear, asking you to confirm the removal. Click Yes or press ⏎.

4. Repeat steps 2–3 to remove more printers.

5. Click Close, or press Tab repeatedly until Close is highlighted and press ⏎ to close the Printers dialog box.

Notes When an installed printer is removed from the list, the printer driver and font files are not deleted from your hard disk. Other printers may use the same driver and/or font files.

Selecting a Printer Port

Your computer has two types of output ports, parallel and serial. The standard DOS machine can have up to three parallel ports and four serial ports, though most computers have only one of each. If you switch your printer from one port to another, you need to use the Control Panel to configure Windows so that it knows it will find the printer on that port.

1. Run the Printers option. The Printers dialog box will appear.

2. Make sure that the printer on the new port is selected. If it is not, click on the printer name (use the scroll arrows if necessary), or use the direction keys to highlight it.

3. Click on the Connect (Alt-C) command button. The Connect dialog box will appear, containing a list box labeled *Ports*.

4. From the Ports list box, select the new printer port.

5. Click on OK or press ↵.

6. When the Printers dialog box reappears, click on Close, or press Tab repeatedly until Close is highlighted and press ↵.

Notes   Windows does not check to see if the port you specify actually exists.

You can also print to a file, rather than a printer. Some computers have a special card installed that enables them to print to certain printers. Use the EPT port in such instances.

Setting Printer Port Options

Once you have selected a port for your installed printer, you can determine how messages will be displayed, how data will be sent to the printer, or if data will be printed directly to the port. See "Options," below, for an explanation of these settings. You can also modify the serial communications settings for your printer port by using the Printer option of the Control Panel.

1. With the Printers dialog box open, click Connect (Alt-C).

2. Press Alt-D (or Tab) to highlight the Device Not Selected text box. Type in the new number.

3. Press Alt-T (or Tab) to highlight the Transmission Retry text box. Type in the new number.

4. If necessary, click on the Fast Printing Direct to Port (Alt-F) check box to disable this option.

5. Click OK or press ↵ to implement these options.

Options
Device Not Selected—the value in the text box is the number of seconds the Print Manager will examine the printer to make sure that it is on and ready for printing. If Print Manager finds

the printer still unavailable by the end of the allotted time, a
message box will appear notifying you of the error.

Transmission Retry—the value in the text box is the number of
seconds the Print Manager will pause before sending a message that the printer cannot receive any additional data for
printing. When the printer has used the data currently in its
memory, it will clear its memory and accept more data. The
default for PostScript printers is 90 seconds; for other printers,
the default is 45 seconds.

Fast Printing Direct to Port—enables Windows to circumvent
DOS and print directly to your printer. Your documents will
print faster.

Notes   If a serial port is selected, Device Not Selected will not
appear as an option.

Setting Serial Port Options

One of the most important concepts to understand about your computer is that of "devices." A device is a part of your computer system from which data can be received or to which data can be sent.
Some of the devices attached to your computer are communications
ports. One of these, the parallel data port, is used with printers. The
other, a serial data port, is used for just about every other peripheral
device on the market—modems, plotters, even robots. Under MS-
DOS, the device name for the serial port is COM1. Any additional
serial ports are named in numeric sequence—COM2, COM3, etc.

Every serial port has several settings associated with it to control
exactly how the port operates. For a serial port to successfully communicate with another serial device, both the device and the port
must be configured with the same settings. Therefore, you may at
times want to change the serial port settings.

1.   Run the Ports option. The Ports dialog box will appear.

2.   Click on the port you wish to configure, or select the port
     by pressing 1 for COM1, 2 for COM2, and so on. Most
     computers have a single serial port called COM1. Win-
     dows will allow you configure ports COM2 through
     COM4 even if they don't exist, however, so be sure to
     determine how many ports your system has.

3. Click Settings (Alt-S). The Settings for COM*n* dialog box appears. Change the desired settings (see "Options," below).

4. Click Advanced (Alt-A) if you wish to change the Base I/O Port Address (Alt-B) or the Interrupt Request Line (Alt-I). To reveal the drop-down list for each option, click on the arrow button or use the key sequence and Alt-↓. Click on the new setting (use the scroll arrows if necessary) or use the direction keys to highlight the new setting and press Alt-↑.

5. Click OK or press ↵. The System Setting Change dialog box appears.

6. If you wish the new setting to take place immediately, you must start Windows again by clicking Restart Now (Alt-R). Otherwise, click Don't Restart Now or press ↵.

7. If you did not restart Windows, click OK or press Tab repeatedly until OK is highlighted and then press ↵.

8. Click Close or press Tab repeatedly until Close is highlighted and then press ↵.

Options

Baud Rate—a measurement of the speed at which serial transmission takes place. It specifies the number of times per second that the serial port changes the voltage of the electric signals it is transmitting.

Data Bits—specifies how many bits constitute a data packet. A bit is a binary digit, either one or zero; it is the unit of information transmitted by the serial port. Data packets are groups of bits used to denote characters and other forms of data. A data packet can be five to eight bits long.

Parity—an error correction scheme used by the serial port. There are five types of parity: even, odd, none, mark, and space. Most systems expect you to use none.

Stop Bits—the specified time unit between data packets (characters). Not bits at all, stop bits are the pauses between bits.

Flow Control—sets the method, or protocol, by which the flow of data is controlled. The choices are Xon/Xoff, Hardware, or None. Xon/Xoff, used by software to control the flow of data,

is a simple protocol that is the default setting for most serial
ports. When Hardware is selected, the serial port control cir-
cuitry handles the information flow. When None is selected, no
flow-control protocol is used.

Setting Up an Installed Printer

Once you have installed a printer, you can change some of the
default printer options such as the size of the paper, the page orientation, and the paper source. See "Setting Up the Printer" under
"Standard Operations."

Installing Printer Fonts

If you are using a printer that requires soft or cartridge fonts, you can
install them using the Font Installer in Printer Setup. Your printer
should already be installed and connected to the correct port.

To install a cartridge font:

1. Click Setup (Alt-S) in the Printers dialog box. The *printer
name* dialog box appears.

2. Click Fonts (Alt-F). The *printer name* Font Installer dialog
box appears.

3. Click the Add Fonts (Alt-A) button.

4. Type in the drive and directory where the fonts you wish
to install are located.

5. Click OK or press ↵. The fonts that are supported will be
displayed in the font list on the right of the *printer name*
Font Installer dialog box.

6. Click on the font name you want or use the direction keys
to highlight it. You can select more than one font. Then
click Add (Alt-A).

7. Type the drive and directory name where the fonts should
be installed.

8. Click OK or press ↵.

9. Click Exit (Alt-X). In the *printer name* dialog box, click on
the name of the cartridge or press Alt-T and use the direction keys to highlight it.

10. Click OK or press ↵ to confirm the printer setup.

11. In the Printers dialog box, click Close or press Tab repeatedly until Close is highlighted and press ↵.

To install a soft font:

1. Click Setup (Alt-S) in the Printers dialog box. The *printer name* dialog box appears.

2. Click Fonts (Alt-F). The *printer name* Font Installer dialog box appears.

3. Click the Add Fonts (Alt-A) button.

4. Type in the drive and directory where the fonts you wish to install are located.

5. Click OK or press ↵. The fonts that are supported will appear in the font list on the right of the *printer name* Font Installer dialog box.

6. Click on the font name you want or use the direction keys to highlight it. You can select more than one font. Then click Add (Alt-A).

7. Type the drive and directory name where the fonts should be installed.

8. Click OK or press ↵. The installed fonts will appear on the left fonts list.

9. Click Exit (Alt-X).

10. In the *printer name* dialog box, click OK or press Tab until OK is highlighted, then press ↵.

11. In the Printers dialog box, click Close or press Tab repeatedly until Close is highlighted and press ↵.

Switching the Default Printer

Windows automatically uses one printer, called the default printer. If you have installed multiple printers for Windows, you will at times need to make a different printer the default printer.

1. Run the Printers option. The Printers dialog box will appear.

2. Move the mouse pointer over the list of installed printers and double-click on the printer you wish to make the default, or click once on the printer and then click on the Set Default Printer command button. Or, use the direction keys to highlight the printer's name and then press Alt-E to designate it the default printer. The name of the default printer, displayed in the Default Printer area, will change.

3. Click on Close, or press Tab repeatedly until Close is highlighted and press ↵.

TrueType Fonts

Windows uses two different types of fonts to display typefaces on-screen, screen fonts and TrueType fonts. A screen font fits the traditional definition of a font: it is a graphic image of a single size of a single typeface—10-point Helvetica, for example. Screen fonts were used with Windows 3.0, and Windows 3.1 continues to support them.

Windows 3.1 also uses a newer type of "font," called a TrueType font. TrueType fonts are scalable. A TrueType font contains the information for a particular typeface that can be enlarged or reduced—scaled—to almost any point size. TrueType fonts allow your text to print as it appears on-screen.

1. Run the Fonts option. The Fonts dialog box will appear.

2. Click on the TrueType command button. The TrueType dialog box will appear.

3. To enable TrueType, click on the Enable TrueType check box. Disable TrueType by clicking on the box a second time. To display *only* TrueType fonts, click on the Show Only TrueType check box. To show both types of fonts, click on the check box a second time to deselect it.

4. Click on OK.

5. When the Fonts dialog box reappears, click on Close.

THE SOUND COMPONENT

In Windows 3.1, the sound options have been enhanced. If your computer has sound devices installed, you can assign a sound file to selected Windows events. The sound file will execute when the event takes place. The Sound component also controls your computer's beep.

1. Run the Sound component of the Control Panel. The Sound dialog box appears.

2. Click on the name of the event you want to accent with a sound file, or use the direction keys to highlight it.

3. In the Files list, click on the sound file you want or press Alt-F and use the direction keys to highlight it. Sound files have a .WAV extension.

4. Click on Test (Alt-T) if you want to hear the sound produced by the sound file.

5. To allow the warning beep and all other assigned sounds (except System Start and System Exit) to be heard, "turn on" the Enable System Sounds check box (the default) by clicking on it or pressing Alt-N. To disable the sounds, remove the X from the check box by using the same method.

6. Click OK or press ↵ to activate the sound selections.

386 ENHANCED MODE

If you have started Windows in 386 Enhanced mode, the 386 Enhanced icon will appear in the Control Panel. With this component of the Control Panel, you can indicate how a non-Windows application will compete with another application for the use of a serial device such as a printer or a modem. You can also specify how you want Windows to perform multitasking.

Adjusting Virtual Memory

1. Run the 386 Enhanced component of the Control Panel. The 386 Enhanced dialog box appears.

2. Click on the Virtual Memory command button (Alt-V) to display the current virtual memory settings.

3. Click Change (Alt-C) if you want to specify new settings. The Virtual Memory dialog box expands to reveal several options.

4. To select a new drive for your swap file, click on the Drive arrow button or press Alt-D and then Alt-↓ to reveal the drive list. Hard drives and network drives will appear on the list. Click on the desired drive letter, or use the direction keys to highlight the drive and press Alt-↑.

5. Click on the arrow button or press Alt-T and then Alt-↓ to select a new Type of swap file. Click on your choice, or use the direction keys to highlight the type and then press Alt-↑. If the drive selected in step 4 is on a network, you cannot select Permanent as the type of swap file.

6. If you want to change the size of the swap file, press Tab or Alt-S to highlight the New Size text box and type in the new number of kilobytes.

7. Click OK or press ↵ to accept your changes.

8. Click OK, or press Tab repeatedly until OK is highlighted.

Notes   Space Available, Maximum Size, and Recommended Size are all informational messages displayed in the expanded Virtual Memory dialog box. The information they provide varies according to the type of swap file selected.

Device Contention

The settings in the Device Contention area of the 386 Enhanced component resolve requests from applications for the simultaneous use of the same device. The device contention options are of concern only when a non-Windows application is involved. Windows applications do not rely on these settings.

1. Run the 386 Enhanced component of the Control Panel. The 386 Enhanced dialog box appears.

2. In the Device Contention area, click on the port assigned to the device in question, or use the direction keys to select the port.

3. Click on the option button or use the key sequence to select Always Warn (Alt-A), Never Warn (Alt-N), or Idle (Alt-I). (See "Options," below.)

4. If you select Idle, you can also choose a new number of seconds for the device to idle. Click on the up arrow to increase or the down arrow to decrease the number of seconds, or press Tab and type in the new number.

5. Click OK or press ⏎ to accept the changes.

Options

Always Warn—displays a message box warning you of a device contention. You must select which application is allowed to use the device.

Never Warn—no message to warn you of a device contention will appear. This option should be selected only if one program at a time is being used on the device: if two programs try to use a single device with this option selected, the output will most likely be unusable.

Idle (in sec.)—specify how long the computer should pause, once a program has finished using a device, before allowing another program to start using the device. No warning message will be displayed. The default is 2 seconds; you can choose any number from 1 through 999.

Scheduling

1. Run the 386 Enhanced component of the Control Panel. The 386 Enhanced dialog box appears.

2. In the Scheduling area, click on the Windows in Fore-
    ground (Alt-F) or the Windows in Background
    (Alt-B) up arrow to increase (or the down arrow to
    decrease) the number of timeslices for each option. Or,
    use the key sequence to highlight the textbox of the
    desired option and type in the new number. The values
    for each option range from 1 through 10,000.

3. If desired, enable the Exclusive in Foreground check box
    by clicking on it or by pressing Alt-E.

4. When necessary, change the value in the Minimum Time-
    slice textbox by clicking on the up arrow to increase or the
    down arrow to decrease the number of milliseconds. Or,
    press Alt-M and type the the new number in the textbox.

5. Click OK or press ↵ to accept your changes.

FILE AND DIRECTORY MANAGEMENT

The File Manager is your most important tool for working with
files and directories. It is an essential component of Windows, and
is run just like any other Windows program. Its icon is in the Main
program group; to run File Manager, start from the Main program
window.

•   Double-click on the File Manager icon, or use the direction
    keys to highlight File Manager and press ↵.

The procedure for closing the File Manager is similar to that for
closing any Windows program, and you have the option of saving
the File Manager configuration when you close the program. If you
choose to save the File Manager's configuration, any changes made
using the Options menu during the current session (file-list display
characteristics and confirmation options) will be preserved.

1. If you wish to preserve the current settings, click on the Options menu (Alt-O) and click Save Settings on Exit (E).

2. Click on File (Alt-F) and click Exit (X), or simply double-click on the Control menu.

CHANGING THE APPEARANCE OF THE FILE MANAGER WINDOW

The File Manager window can be minimized when you use the File Manager to run an application, and you can choose to display (the default) or suppress the status bar.

1. Click Options (Alt-O) to pull down the Options menu.

2. If you wish to suppress the File Manager window's status bar, select Status Bar (S). To redisplay the status bar, repeat steps 1–2.

3. If you wish File Manager to be minimized when you run an application, repeat step 1 and select Minimize on Use (M).

Notes   With a directory highlighted in the directory list, the status bar indicates the total amount of space in kilobytes on the selected drive, the amount of free space, and the number and size in bytes of files in the selected directory. When one or more files in the contents list are highlighted, the status bar indicates the number and size in bytes of the files selected, and the total number and the size in bytes of files of the directory.

Changing the Appearance of the Drive Window

You will notice that the File Manager window contains another window, the currently selected drive window. This window (usually your Windows directory) reacts to commands in the same way as do other windows. It can be moved, resized, or minimized to an icon. In Windows 3.1, however, it differs from other windows in that it is divided into two "panes" (the default). The left pane contains the directory tree, and the right pane contains the contents of the selected directory, including subdirectories.

The appearance of the File Manager window can be changed to suit your needs. You can choose to resize the panes, display either the directory tree pane or the contents pane, display only certain types of files, or sort the files in any of several different ways.

Adjusting the Directory Window Panes

The directory window can be divided into two panes. The size of displayed panes can also be adjusted.

1. With the tree and directory panes displayed (the default), click and hold the line to the right of the directory tree pane vertical scroll bar. The line becomes a vertical bar, and the mouse pointer becomes a two-headed arrow intersected by a vertical line. Or, pull down the View (Alt-V) menu and select Split (Alt-L) to make the vertical bar appear.

2. Move the pointer to the left to increase the size of the contents pane and to decrease the size of the tree pane, or to the right to increase the size of the directory tree pane and decrease the size of the contents pane. When the panes are displayed in the sizes you require, release the mouse button. Or, use the direction keys to move the vertical bar and press ⅃ to select the new pane sizes.

Notes   If you are currently displaying only the directory tree pane or the current contents pane, the line to click and hold with the mouse is on the far right side of the directory window.

Changing Directory and Contents List Views

You can choose to display the directory tree only, the contents of the current directory only, or both the directory tree and the contents list. These options are available from the File Manager's menu bar on the View (Alt-V) pull-down menu. Only one option can be selected at a time; the selected option is indicated by a check mark.

Options

Tree and Directory (Alt-R)—the default, this displays both the directory tree and the current contents of the selected directory.

Tree Only (Alt-E)—displays only the directory tree of the current drive.

Directory Only (Alt-O)—displays only the current contents of the selected directory.

Displaying Selected Files

You can choose to display different groups of files in the currently selected directory.

1. On the File Manager menu bar, click View (Alt-V) to display the pull-down menu and click By File Type (T). The By File Type dialog box appears.

2. In the Name (Alt-N) text box, use wildcard characters to select the display of file names with similar characteristics. This selection will override any other options you can select for file display (see "Options," below).

3. Or, if you wish, enable the check box (the default for all groups except hidden/system files) for each group you wish displayed.

Options

Directories (Alt-D)—the subdirectories of the currently selected directory.

Programs (Alt-P)—files with an .EXE, .COM, .PIF, or .BAT extension.

Documents (Alt-M)—the files associated with a program.

Other Files (Alt-O)—all files that are not subdirectories, programs, documents, or hidden/system files.

Show Hidden/System Files (Alt-S)—when enabled, hidden/system files will be displayed in the contents list. The default is disabled.

Notes   To allow the options to be displayed, the Name text box should indicated all files (*.*). If you change the file specification in the Name text box, only the specified files will appear in the contents list, regardless of the options you have enabled.

Showing File Information

If the contents list of the current directory is displayed in the directory window, you can specify how much file information you wish the contents list to include. In addition to the names of the files and subdirectories (the default), you can specify that the file size, most recent modification date and time, and attributes be displayed.

1. To display all file details, click on View (Alt-V) and select All File Details (Alt-A). The file size, date and time it was last saved, and the file attribute are displayed for each file in the list. The date and time of creation of each subdirectory is also displayed.

2. To return to a display that includes only file and subdirectory names (the default), click View (Alt-V) and select Name (N).

To display selected file information:

1. Click View (Alt-V) and select Partial Details (Alt-P). The Partial Details dialog box appears.

2. Disable the check box for each file detail you do not wish to display in the contents list by clicking on it or by using the key sequence. (See "Options," below.)

3. Click OK or press ↵ to display the enabled file details.

Options

Size (Alt-S)—the number of kilobytes in the file.

Last Modification Date (Alt-M)—the date the file was last saved.

Last Modification Time (Alt-T)—the time the file was last saved.

File Attributes (Alt-A)—denotes whether the file is designated read only, hidden, system, or archive file. Hidden and system file will not appear in the list by default. See "Displaying Selected Files."

Sorting Files and Subdirectories

The list of files and subdirectories appears in alphabetical order in the contents list. If you prefer, you can choose to display the file names by type, date, or size. (See "Options," below.) Only one option can be selected at a time; a check mark will appear beside the selected option.

To change the order of the files in the contents list, click View (Alt-V), then click on the desired option. The subdirectories are listed first in each display.

Options

Sort by Name (Alt-S)—the file and subdirectory names are listed in alphabetical order (the default).

Sort by Type (Alt-B)—the files are listed in alphabetical order, by their extensions.

Sort by Size (Alt-Z)—files are listed from largest to smallest.

Sort by Date (Alt-D)—files are listed by the last date they were saved and subdirectories are listed by their creation dates. The most recent files and subdirectories appear at the top of the list.

Notes   If the Save Settings on Exit option is selected, the selected file sorting option will be in effect each time you reopen File Manager.

DIRECTORY AND DISK DRIVE OPERATIONS

Changing Disk Drives

File Manager is used to manage all the drives installed in or connected to your computer, and it allows you to switch drives and address those drives. Once you switch drives, the drive and directory information in the current directory window will be replaced by the new drive's information. You can also change disk drives and generate a new directory window. See "Opening a Directory Window."

- Click on the icon of the drive you want, or press Ctrl-
  Drive. (Remember, *Drive* specifies a drive letter of your
  choosing.) Or, click on Disk (Alt-D) in the File Manager
  menu bar, click Select Drive (S), and then double-click on
  the drive letter in the Drives list or use the direction keys
  to highlight the drive letter and press ⏎. You can also
  change disk drives by pressing Tab repeatedly until the
  currently selected drive is highlighted, using the direction
  keys to highlight the new drive, and then pressing ⏎.

Collapsing a Directory Tree

The File Manager allows you to "collapse" a directory so that you see only the directory levels you want. When a tree or a branch of a tree is collapsed, the directories on the levels below that of the current directory disappear from the screen. If you have enabled the display of expanded directories (see "Displaying an Expanded Directory Tree"), the symbol inside the current directory's icon changes from a minus sign to a plus sign.

- Click on the directory icon in the level directly above that
  of the subdirectories you no longer wish to see, or highlight the icon by using the direction keys. Click on Tree
  (Alt-T) and Collapse Branch (C), or press the minus key (–).
  Or, double-click on a folder to collapse everything beneath
  that level into the folder.

Creating a New Directory

You can create a new subdirectory of the current directory, or, by specifying a path, any directory you wish.

1. Pull down the File menu (Alt-F). Select Create Directory (E). The Create Directory dialog box appears.

2. The current directory path appears on the Current Directory information line. To make a subdirectory of the currently selected directory, type a new name in the Name (Alt-N) text box.

3. To create a subdirectory of a different directory, type the path in the Name text box.

4. Click OK or press ↵. The new directory or subdirectory will appear in the directory list.

Creating a System Disk

A system disk is a disk that contains the DOS files necessary for booting your computer. You can add the system files to a diskette using the Disk menu option in File Manager. See "Formatting a Diskette " for instructions.

Notes   If there is no room for the system files on the diskette, or if the disk is not formatted, the System Disk Error message box will appear. Click OK or press ↵ to remove the message box, then insert a different formatted diskette into the drive before redoing these steps.

Displaying an Expanded Directory Tree

By default, File Manager doesn't indicate if there are subdirectories beneath the directory folders in the directory tree pane. However, you can configure the File Manager to place symbols in a directory folder to show whether there are subdirectories beneath it.

A plus sign appears in a directory folder to indicate that that directory has subdirectories. A minus sign appears in a directory folder to indicate that its subdirectories are currently listed in the directory tree pane.

- Click on Tree (Alt-T) in the File Manager's menu bar, then click Indicate Expandable Branches (I).

Notes   To retain this configuration permanently, configure File Manager to save its settings upon exiting. See the instructions for closing File Manager under "File and Directory Management."

Expanding a Directory Tree

The File Manager displays directory structures in the form of an "inverted tree" diagram, in the directory tree pane of each directory window. Each directory is represented by the symbol of a folder, called a directory icon. Some subdirectories—"branches" of the tree—may not be visible. This is not because they've scrolled off the bottom of the window; it's because the File Manager has displayed only the first level of subdirectories, in order to make the tree as a whole easier to view. (In the File Manager's default state, you can't determine by looking at the directory icons if there are subdirectories beneath them. But if you like, you can configure the File Manager to place symbols in a directory folder to indicate whether there are subdirectories beneath it. See "Displaying an Expanded Directory Tree.")

You can make subdirectories visible by expanding a single level of a branch on the tree, an entire branch, or the entire tree. There is a difference between expanding one level and expanding a branch: the former displays only those subdirectories *immediately* below the highlighted directory, while the latter displays *all* subdirectories below the highlighted directory.

- Use the direction keys to highlight the directory you wish to expand. Pull down Tree (Alt-T) and select Expand One Level (X) or Expand Branch (B).

Labeling a Disk

You may wish to add or modify the volume label on a hard or floppy disk. File Manager allows you to make this change using the Disk menu. The volume label can be up to 11 characters long.

1. Activate the drive window for the disk drive containing the disk you wish to label.

2. Click Disk (Alt-D) and select Label Disk (L). The Label Disk dialog box appears.

3. If the disk currently has a label, it will appear in the Label text box. Type the new label in the Label (Alt-L) text box.

4. Click OK or press ↵. The new label will be copied to the disk.

Opening a Directory Window

A directory window is a document window that appears inside the File Manager. The default setting divides each directory window into two parts, or panes: the directory tree pane on the left side, and the contents list pane on the right side. The file list contains a list of the files in the current directory, which is highlighted in the directory tree. When you select a new directory in the directory tree pane, the information in the contents list pane changes.

From the contents list pane, you can select one or more files and change their attributes, move them between directories, or open, run, print, rename, delete, or copy them.

When you first run the File Manager, a directory window appears. That window will contain drive and directory information for either the Windows directory or the drive and directory last in use when the Save Settings on Exit option was selected.

The most efficient way to use the File Manager is to generate multiple directory windows, and then move or copy files between them. To open additional directory windows, follow these instructions:

- Double-click on the icon of the drive for which you want a new directory window. Or, pull down the Window menu (Alt-W), select New Window (N), then change the window information to reflect a new drive by pressing Ctrl-*Drive*. (*Drive* specifies a drive letter of your choosing.)

Selecting an Active Drive Window

When more than one drive window is open, it may be necessary to select a drive window or icon that is not the currently active window. There are several ways to accomplish this:

- Click anywhere in the directory window you wish to make active.

- Press Ctrl-F6 to move among the open directory windows.

- Select Window (Alt-W) to pull down the Window menu, and then select the desired window from the list by pressing the assigned number.

FILE OPERATIONS

Changing File Attributes

The File Manager contains a command for allowing you to view and change the attributes of a file or a group of files.

1. Click on the file name in the contents list, or use the direction keys to highlight it.

2. Click File (Alt-F) to pull down the menu and select Properties (T), or press Alt-↵. The Properties for *Filename* dialog box will appear. The top portion of the dialog box displays information about the selected file(s). If only one file is selected, the dialog box will list the file name, size, date of last change, and the path where the file is located. If more than one file is selected, the text appears as the number of selected files and the total size of the files in bytes.

3. The file's attribute is shown by the marked check box in the Attributes area of the dialog box. (If more than one file is selected, only the attributes shared by all selected files will be enabled.) To change the file attribute, disable the current attribute by clicking on the check box or by using the key sequence. (See "Options," below.) Enable the new attribute in the same way.

4. Click OK or press ↵.

Options

Read Only (Alt-R)—prevents a file from being altered.

Archive (Alt-A)—stamps a file that has been modified since it was last backed up. This attribute is helpful if you use the DOS Backup, Restore, and Xcopy commands.

Hidden (Alt-I)—prevents hidden files, which do not normally appear in the file list of a directory, from being deleted or over-written.

System (Alt-S)—marks a file as being a DOS system file. System files usually do not appear on the file list.

Notes Hidden and system files can be displayed in the File Manager by selecting View (Alt-V), By File Type (T), and then enabling the Show Hidden/System (Alt-S) files check box.

Copying a Diskette

You can copy the contents of one diskette to another by using the Copy option on the File Manager's Disk menu. This option works in the same way as the DOS Diskcopy command. The contents of the source diskette replace the contents of the target diskette. The diskettes must be exactly the same size and type. When an unformatted diskette is used, it will be formatted to the same size as the source diskette before the source contents are copied to it. The Copy option can be used to make a backup copy of the contents of a diskette.

1. Insert the diskette you wish to copy (the source) into the floppy-disk drive. If you are copying to a second floppy-disk drive, insert the diskette you wish to copy to (the target).

2. Activate the drive icon for the source diskette (see "Changing Disk Drives").

3. Click Disk (Alt-D), and select Copy Disk (C). If you have two floppy-disk drives, the Copy Disk dialog box appears. If you have only one floppy-disk drive, the dialog box is not displayed.

4. If the Copy Disk dialog box appears, select the source diskette by clicking on the arrow button or pressing Alt-↓ to reveal the drop-down list in the Source In (Alt-S) list box.

Click on the drive letter, or use the direction keys to high-light it and press Alt-↑.

5. In the Copy Disk dialog box, select a target drive by clicking on the Destination In arrow button, or by pressing Alt-D and then Alt-↓ to reveal the target drive list box. Click on the drive letter, or use the direction keys to highlight it and press Alt-↑.

6. In the Copy Disk dialog box, click OK or press ↵.

7. The Confirm Copy Disk message box appears. Click Yes or press ↵ to replace the contents of the target diskette with the source diskette data.

8. When the Copy Disk message box appears, click OK or press ↵.

9. The Copying Disk dialog box appears, to inform you of the progress of your diskette copy process. When prompted, insert your destination diskette and then click OK or press ↵. When the copy is complete, the Copying Disk message box disappears from your screen.

Notes   You may wish to suppress the confirmation message mentioned in step 7. See "Displaying Confirmation Messages."

Copying or Moving a File or Directory

Using the File Manager, you can copy or move a file (or several files) or a directory in various ways. After selecting files with the mouse or the keyboard, use the File pull-down menu for either operation. Or, in Windows 3.1, the newly implemented drag-and-drop method allows you to "drag" the file(s) to a new drive or directory and "drop" the selected data in the new location.

Both individual files and entire directories can be copied or moved.

Using the Drag-and-Drop Method

The File Manager lets you copy or move files and directories in a very simple, visual way that is far superior to the standard DOS command line. You simply open the directory window containing the file. Then, you "drag" the file from that window to its destination—another drive icon, another directory folder in the current or another directory window, or to a file list in a different directory window. You can also copy or move a file to a minimized directory window. Start the copying or moving operation by making sure the destination directory, whether it's a file list or a directory window icon, is visible on the File Manager workspace.

1. Open the directory windows that contain the source and the destination of the file or directory. (A directory window that is minimized as an icon is open.)

2. Click and hold the file(s) or directory icons you wish to copy or move.

    • To copy a file or directory to a new directory on the same drive, press the Ctrl key while dragging the file or directory icon to the new directory.

    • To copy a file or directory to a new drive, drag its icon to the new drive window icon or drag the icon to the directory window or the directory window icon.

    • To move a file or directory to a new drive on the same directory, drag the file or directory icon to the new directory.

    • To move a file or directory to a different drive, press the Shift key while dragging the file or directory icon to the drive window, drive window icon, or drive letter icon.

3. The Confirm Mouse Operation message box appears. Click Yes or press ↵. If you are replacing a file with another file of the same name, the Confirm Replace message box appears. Click Yes or press ↵ to replace the file.

4. The Copying or Moving dialog box appears. You can cancel copying or moving the file by clicking Cancel or pressing ↵.

Notes   You can suppress the confirming messages. See "Displaying Confirmation Messages."

If you copy or move a directory and its files and subdirectories to a different drive by using the drag-and-drop method, the directory and subdirectories will automatically be created on the new drive.

Using the Keyboard

You can also copy or move files from the keyboard. If you are copying files, you can choose to copy them to the Clipboard.

1. Click on the file name or use the direction keys to highlight it.

2. Click File (Alt-F) and then select Copy (C), or press the F8 key to copy a file or directory. Select File and then Move (M), or press the F7 key to move a file or directory.

3. The Copy or Move dialog box appears with the name of the selected file or directory in the From (Alt-F) text box. You can type in another file name if you wish. Type the destination path in the To (Alt-T) text box. If you are copying a directory, a message box will appear asking if you wish to create the specified directory on the new drive.

4. To copy or move the file or directory, click OK or press ⏎. The status of the copy or move appears in the dialog box. When the file is copied or moved, the dialog box disappears.

Creating a Program Icon

The File Manager and Program Manager are designed to interact so that you can create a program icon in a very easy, visual way. The process is similar to that of copying files using the drag-and-drop method, except that in this case you "copy" a program file directly from the File Manager into a group window of the Program Manager.

1. Place the File Manager and Program Manager windows on the desktop at the same time.

2. Size the windows so that they each take up half of the desktop. You might want to tile them using the Task List. (See "Tiling and Cascading Application Windows" in Part I.)

3. In the Program Manager, open the destination group window.

4. In the File Manager, select the directory folder that contains the program file name.

5. Click and hold the program file in the contents list pane, and drag the file into the destination group window in Program Manager.

6. Release the mouse button. (You may be prompted to select the correct application name to assign to the icon. Click on a name in the list and then click OK.) An icon for the selected program will appear. If the program is a standard DOS program, the icon will be a blue box with the words *MS DOS* in it.

See Also   Adding a Program to a Group

Deleting a File or Directory

In most circumstances, File Manager lets you delete any file on any disk. The exception to this is network disk drives, where you may be restricted from deleting certain files if you are not at the required privilege level.

The File Manager will also allow you to delete entire directories and their subdirectories, including all the files in them.

1. Click on the name of the file or directory you wish to delete. Or, press Tab to move the cursor to the correct pane and use the direction keys to highlight the file or directory.

2. Click on File (Alt-F) and select Delete (D), or press the Delete key. The Delete dialog box appears.

3. To delete the file or directory whose name appears in the Delete (Alt-L) text box, click OK or press ⏎. To delete a different file or directory, type the name (including the path if the file is in a different directory) in the Delete text box. Then click OK or press CR.

4. The Confirm File Delete or Confirm Directory Delete message box appears. Click Yes or press ⏎ to confirm the directory and/or file deletion. If you have selected a group of files, click Yes to All or press Alt-A.

Notes You can suppress the Confirm File Delete and the Confirm Directory Delete message boxes. See "Displaying Confirmation Messages."

If you have selected more than one file to delete, the text box in the Delete dialog box will display as many names as will fit.

Displaying Confirmation Messages

Confirmation message boxes appear when you are deleting a file or directory, copying or moving files with the mouse, and replacing a file with a file of the same name. By default, each option is enabled. The confirmation messages let you know which command you have selected, and allow you to escape if you have not selected the command you wished to use. Any or all of the messages can be suppressed.

1. Click Options (Alt-O) and select Confirmation (C). The Confirmation dialog box appears.

2. Click on the option or press the key sequence to disable any Confirm On option whose message box you wish to suppress (see "Options," below). You can enable the options again by repeating this step.

3. Click OK or press ↵ to accept your changes.

Options

File Delete (Alt-D)—displays a message box when a file is deleted.

Directory Delete (Alt-I)—displays a message when a directory is selected for deletion. When a directory is deleted, all its files and subdirectories are also deleted.

File Replace (Alt-R)—displays a message box to inform you that a file is being overwritten.

Mouse Actions (Alt-M)—displays the confirmation message box when files are moved or copied by using the drag-and-drop method.

Disk Commands (Alt-K)—displays the confirmation message box when the Disk menu options are used.

Printing with the File Manager

File Manager allows you to print document files in two different ways. Document files are those that have been associated with an application. (See "Associating File Types with Applications.") Document files appear in the contents list pane with an icon that looks like a small piece of paper with lines on it.

1. Run the Print Manager and minimize it to an icon.

2. From the File Manager directory window, click on the document file you wish to print and, while holding down the mouse button, "drag" the file icon onto the Print Manager icon.

3. Release the mouse button to "drop" the file in the Print Manager. The Print Manager will print the file in the usual way. (See "Print Manager Operations.")

Or,

1. Click on the document file you wish to print in the contents list pane, or use the direction keys to highlight the file.

2. Click File (Alt-F) and select Print (P). The Print dialog box will appear.

3. The directory of the selected file is shown in the Current Directory message. If you wish to print a different file, type the file's path (if the file is in a different directory) and name in the Print (Alt-P) text box.

4. When the file you wish to print appears in the Print text box, click OK or press ↵. The Print Manager will automatically run and print the file in the usual way.

Notes If the document you wish to print was generated using Write, the Print dialog box will appear. You can specify the number of copies to print, the range of pages to include, whether to print the document to a file instead of the printer, and, with some printers, the printing resolution. You can also change the printer setup options.

Renaming a File

File Manager lets you rename any file or directory, as long as the new name follows DOS file-naming conventions.

Start with an open directory window that contains the file or directory you want to rename.

1. Click on the file or directory you want to rename, or use the direction keys to highlight it.

2. Click on File (Alt-F) and select Rename (N). The Rename dialog box appears.

3. The path of the selected file or directory appears in the Current Directory message line. The name of the selected file or directory is in the From text box. Type a new name for the selected file or directory in the To (Alt-T) text box.

4. Click OK or press ↵.

Notes   You can rename a group of files by selecting them and invoking the renaming procedure described above. When the Rename dialog box appears, instead of keying in a single file name, type a wildcard specification in the To text box. For example, if you select ten files, you can rename them all so that they have a .BAK extension. When the Rename dialog box appears, simply type *.BAK and press ↵.

Searching for Files or Subdirectories

In File Manager, you can locate a file, a group of files, or subdirectories by conducting a search. The file or subdirectory location is displayed in the Search Results window.

The Search Results window can be resized, minimized, or closed the same way as any other window. When it is open, it appears in the list of open windows in the Window pull-down menu. Many File Manager commands can be used with files appearing in the Search Results window, but you cannot move or copy any other files into the window. When you search for a new group of files, the contents of the Search Results window are replaced with the new files.

1. Click on the directory you wish to search or use the direction keys to highlight it. Or, select a file whose name contains the extension you wish to search for.

2. Click File (Alt-F) and select Search (H). The Search dialog box appears.

3. Type a file name in the Search For (Alt-S) text box to reveal the location of a single file. Or, use wildcards to specify file names or extensions to search for. (If a file name is selected in the contents list pane, the file's extension will be the specification in the Search For text box. If no file name is selected, the search specification will be all files.)

4. In the Search From (Alt-F) text box, type the letter of the drive where you wish to begin the search.

5. To include subdirectories of the selected directory in the search, leave the Search All Subdirectories option enabled. To search only the selected directory, disable the option by clicking on its check box or by pressing Alt-E.

6. Click OK or press ↵ to perform the search. If there are files that match the search specifications, they will be listed in the Search Results window. The Search Results message box will inform you if no files match the search specifications. Click OK to remove the message box.

Selecting a File

To select a file is to highlight it, which tells the File Manager to make it the object of whatever action you next initiate. You can select multiple files and perform actions on them. A selected file name appears in reverse video.

Every active directory window has at least one directory or file selected. When the directory window opens, the first directory (or file, if there are no directories) in the list is selected. To select a file:

1. If your window displays a directory list, select the appropriate directory by clicking on the directory name, or use the direction keys to move the selection cursor from name to name.

2. Click on the file you wish to select, or use the direction
keys to make your selection.

See Also Selecting Multiple Files

Selecting Multiple Files

File Manager allows you to select entire groups of files and perform
operations on them. You can select groups of consecutive files,
which are files that appear one after the other in the directory window list; or you can select nonconsecutive groups of files, such as
the fourth, the tenth, then the fourteenth file in the list. To select
multiple files, start with an open directory window.

To Select All Files

• Press Ctrl-/. To deselect the files, press Spacebar.

To Select Consecutive Files

1. Click on the first file in the series, or use the direction keys
to highlight it.

2. Move the mouse pointer to the last file in the series, press
and hold the Shift key, and click on the last file name. Or,
press the Shift key while using the direction keys to highlight the series of files. All the files in the series will be
selected.

To Select Nonconsecutive Files

1. Click on the first file you wish to select, or use the direction keys to highlight the file.

2. Press the Ctrl key and click on the next file name you wish
to select. Or, press and release the Shift-F8 key, and use the
direction keys to move the cursor. The cursor becomes a
blinking dotted rectangle. When it surrounds the file you
wish to select, press Spacebar.

3. Repeat step 2 for each file you wish to select. When you
have finished selecting files by using the direction keys,
press Shift-F8 again.

Notes This is useful when you need to scroll through a large number of files and select only some of them.

See Also Copying or Moving a File or Directory

FORMATTING A DISKETTE

At times you will need to prepare floppy disks to receive data. File Manager allows you to do this. The File Manager Format command allows you three options when formatting a disk:

Label—You can choose to attach a volume label, which is simply a name for a disk, to the disk you format. A volume label cannot exceed 11 characters in length. The volume label will be displayed by the File Manager and by most other disk management programs whenever they access the disk.

System Disk—You can choose to make the disk a system disk. A system disk is one from which your computer can start, or *boot*. The system files on your hard disk contain information the computer needs each time you start it. You can place these files on a diskette, which will then be available for starting the computer if the hard disk isn't working or if you need to bypass it for any reason.

Quick Format—The Quick Format works with previously formatted disks. When Quick Format is selected, File Manager doesn't really format the disk; instead, it wipes out the directory and file information on disk, rendering it blank far more quickly than a standard format procedure would.

To format a disk:

1. Place the disk you wish to format in the disk drive.

2. Click on Disk (Alt-D) and select Format Disk (F). The Format Disk dialog box will appear.

3. If the Disk In drop-down list box (Alt-D) does not show the correct drive, click the arrow button or press Alt-D and then Alt-↓ to reveal the drop-down list. Click on the drive letter, or use the direction keys to select it and then press Alt-↑.

4. If the Capacity drop-down list box (Alt-C) does not show the capacity of the disk you are formatting (if you have 720KB disk in the drive, for example, but the list box shows 1.44MB), then pull down the drop-down list (as in step 3) and select the correct capacity.

5. To create a volume label, select the Label text box (Alt-L) and type the desired text.

6. Click the Make System Disk (Alt-M) and/or Quick Format (Alt-Q) check boxes or use the key sequence to enable the desired options.

7. Click on OK or press ⏎. A dialog box will appear asking if you really want to format the disk.

8. Click Yes or press ⏎. The disk will be formatted.

THE HELP SYSTEM

To aid you in understanding and using Windows, Microsoft has provided one of the most advanced help facilities available, called simply Windows Help. Help does not appear as a Program Item icon in a group window. Instead, Windows Help is accessible at any time from within almost every Windows program.

There are four methods for invoking Help:

• Pull down the Help menu (Alt-H) and click on the desired menu option, or use the ↑ and ↓ keys to highlight the option, then press ⏎. Windows Help will run, the Help text file for the currently active program will be loaded into it, and the Help program will go directly to the portion of the Help text file you specified—Contents, Search for Help on, How to Use Help, or About.

• Click on a Help Command button in a dialog box, if available.

• Press the F1 key.

• Press the Shift-F1 key sequence.

Shift-F1 and Help Command buttons are available only under certain circumstances, as explained in "Notes," below.

Windows Help appears on your screen in a window, which can be used in the same ways as other windows: it can be moved, resized, minimized to an icon, or closed. There are several ways to close the Help window:

- Double-click on the Control menu icon
- Pull down the Control menu by clicking once on the icon or by pressing Alt-Spacebar, then select Close (C)
- Press Alt-F4
- Pull down the File (Alt-F) menu and select Exit (X)

Notes   Some dialog boxes have a Help Command button; you can access Windows Help by clicking on this button. Help text concerning the currently active dialog box will appear.

Press the F1 key when you are working with an application and Windows Help will display the Help Index file for that program. Some Windows programs will display Help on a menu or dialog box option, or in a system message box when the F1 key is pressed.

Some Windows programs implement an advanced Help feature. To use this feature, hold down the Shift and F1 keys. A question mark appears beside the mouse pointer. You can move the mouse pointer/question mark around on the screen and select a menu option or press a key sequence to bring up the Help text for that specific option or sequence. None of the applications that are included with Windows use this feature.

ACCESSING THE TABLE OF CONTENTS

The tables of contents for most Windows help files are organized under three main headings: How To, Commands, and Keyboard. Individual programs can have more headings or headings with different names.

The following instructions describe how to access the Help table of contents from inside Windows Help. You can also jump to the Help table of contents directly from an application's Help menu by clicking Help (Alt-H) on the menu bar, then selecting Contents (C).

• Click on the Contents button, or press C. The current Help file's table of contents will appear.

ADDING A NOTE TO A HELP TOPIC

Sometimes you will find it useful to add your own comments to a Help topic. Annotate, an option on the Help window's Edit menu, allows you to inspect your notes and copy them to another Help topic or to a document.

1. Click Edit (Alt-E) and select Annotate (A). The Annotate dialog box appears.

2. Type your note in the Annotation (Alt-A) text box. Use the Backspace key to delete typographical errors, and, if necessary, ↵ to begin a new line.

3. Click Save (Alt-S) to save your note and remove the Annotate dialog box. A paper clip will appear before the Help topic's title to indicate an annotation.

Copying or Pasting a Note

You can copy text from your notes or from another document into a Help topic annotation, and you can paste text from your annotations into another note or a document. To copy text from a note:

1. Click on the paper clip in front of the Help topic's title, or press Tab to select the paper clip and then press ↵. The Annotate dialog box will appear.

2. Select the text to copy by clicking and dragging the mouse, or use the Shift key with the direction keys to highlight the text. If you want to copy the entire note, you do not have to highlight the text.

3. Click Copy or press Alt-C. The selected text is copied to the Clipboard.

4. Click Save or press Alt-S to remove the Annotate dialog box.

To paste text from the Clipboard into a note:

1. Select the Help topic where you wish to paste the text.

2. Click on the paper clip in front of the Help topic's title or press Tab to select the paper clip. If no paper clip is visible, click Edit (Alt-E) and then select Annotate (A). The Annotate dialog box will appear.

3. If necessary, click on the place where you wish to paste the text, or use the direction keys to move the insertion point. Click Paste (Alt-P). The Clipboard contents are inserted in the note.

4. Click Save (Alt-S).

Notes Copying and pasting text from a document requires the same steps as above. See "Clipboard Operations" for additional information.

CALLING UP REFERENCES AND DEFINITIONS

Some of the text that appears in the Help window is underlined, either with a solid or a dotted line. If you are using a color monitor, both the text and the line are green. The text that is underlined with a solid line is a *reference,* or a word or phrase for which there is further explanatory Help text. The dotted underline means that definitions for the underlined text are available. You can call up references and definitions with the mouse or with the keyboard:

•   To call up either a reference or a definition, click on the underlined text. Or, press Tab repeatedly until the desired text is highlighted, then press ↵.

To remove a definition box, click anywhere on the screen or press any key.

CREATING A BOOKMARK

A *bookmark* in Windows Help terminology is a location marker placed at any Help topic. Markers are given names, which appear under the Bookmark menu and are numbered sequentially starting with 1.

Start from the Help topic that you wish to mark.

1. Click Bookmark (Alt-M) and select Define (D). The Bookmark Define dialog box appears.

2. The current Help topic title appears in the Bookmark Name (Alt-B) text box. If you wish to assign a new name to the current topic, type a new name in the text box.

3. Click OK or press ↵ to mark the current Help topic.

DELETING A BOOKMARK

Once you have used a bookmark a few times, you will probably memorize its subject matter and no longer need it. At that point, you can delete the bookmark.

Start from the Help text file containing the bookmark you wish to delete.

1. Click Bookmark (Alt-M) and select Define (D). The Bookmark Define dialog box appears.

2. Click on the Help topic name in the list box (use the scroll arrows if necessary), or press Tab to move the highlight to the list box and use the direction keys to highlight the Help topic.

3. Click Delete (Alt-D). The Help topic name is removed from the list box.

4. Repeat steps 2–3 until each bookmark you wish to delete is removed.

5. Click Cancel or press Tab repeatedly until Cancel is highlighted to remove the Bookmark Define dialog box.

GOING BACK TO A HELP SCREEN

Windows Help keeps a record of the Help text you've requested. You can go back along the path you've traveled by using the Back button or the History button, both available on the Help window button bar.

To Use the Back Button

Start from anywhere in the Help system, except at the very first screen that appears when you invoke Help. (You can't move backward if you haven't moved forward yet.)

- Click on the Back button or press Alt-B. Windows Help will move to the Help screen that appeared prior to the current one.

To Use the History Button

Windows Help will show a list of all the references you have viewed in the current Help session. You can then select one of those references and jump back to it, using the History button.

1. Click on the History button or press Alt-T. Windows Help will display a window listing all the previously viewed references.

2. Double-click on the reference of your choice, or move to it using the ↑ and ↓ keys and then press ↵.

KEEPING THE HELP TOPIC DISPLAYED

There may be times when you want the selected Help topic to appear on top of other open windows on the desktop, even if you are using another application. For example, you may need the appropriate Help topic to assist you in the performance of some seldom-used command. If you wish, you can use the Always on Top option available on the Help pull-down menu. When Always on Top is selected, a dark edge is displayed around the Help window border.

From the Help window:

1. Click Help (Alt-H) to pull down the Help menu.

2. Click Always on Top (T) to enable the option. Repeat these steps to disable Always on Top.

OPENING A HELP FILE

You can open a Windows application Help file from any other Help window using the Open command on the File pull-down menu. See "Opening a File" under "Standard Operations."

SEARCHING ON A KEYWORD

You can search the current Help text file for specific words or topics by using the Search button. Once invoked, the Search button brings up the Search dialog box pictured in Figure II.9.

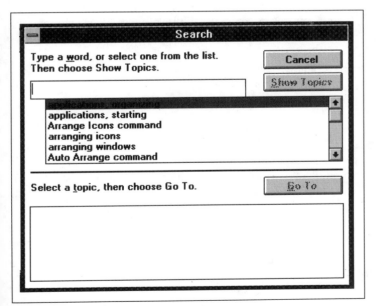

Figure II.9: The Search dialog box

Start from anywhere in the Windows Help program.

1. Click on the the Search button or press Alt-S. The Search dialog box will appear. Within the Search dialog box is a text box and two list boxes. One list box is filled with keywords, which are common words or phrases linked to a specific Help file topic. The text box is where you type in the keyword for which you wish to search. By default, it contains the first word in the keyword list box.

2. Type in the word or phrase for which you wish to search. As you type, Windows Help will move through the list of keywords, displaying the word that most closely matches what you are typing. If the word you are searching for appears in the list box, you can simply click the mouse pointer on it to select it. If you don't have a mouse, continue typing the word or phrase until it is highlighted in the keyword list box.

3. After you have selected a keyword from the list or have finished typing the keyword in the text box, click on the Show Topics command button or press Alt-S. The Help topics that contain the specified keyword will appear in the lower list box.

4. Double-click on the topic you wish to see. Or, highlight the topic using the direction keys, then click on Go To (Alt-G) or press ↵.

SELECTING A BOOKMARK

When you create a bookmark, the name of the bookmark is added to a numbered list on the Bookmark pull-down menu. Up to nine bookmarks can appear on the list. If more bookmarks are defined, an additional option called More appears on the Bookmark pull-down menu. To select a bookmark from the list:

1. Click Bookmark (Alt-M) to pull down the Bookmark menu.

2. Click on the defined bookmark name or press the number that corresponds to the bookmark's name.

3. If the bookmark does not appear in the numbered list and the More option is on the pull-down menu, click on More (M). The Bookmark dialog box will appear.

4. Double-click on the desired bookmark name in the Go To Bookmark (Alt-G) list box to display the corresponding Help topic. Or, use the direction keys to highlight the book-mark name and press ↵. The dialog box will disappear and the selected Help topic will be displayed.

USING THE GLOSSARY

The Windows Help glossary is a text file containing definitions of all the special terms associated with Windows. You can call up the glossary whenever you are in Windows Help (except when you are in How To Use Help) by using the Glossary button.

1. Click on the Glossary button or press Alt-G. The Glossary window will appear.

2. Click on the word or phrase you wish defined, or press Tab until the word or phrase is selected and then press ↵. Windows Help will display a definition.

3. Click again or press any key to close the definition box.

4. Exit the Glossary window by double-clicking on the Control icon. Or, press Alt-Spacebar to reveal the Control menu and select Close (C). You can also exit by pressing Alt-F4.

THE MACRO RECORDER

The Windows Recorder is a program that records keystrokes and mouse movements and plays them back at a later time. Using Recorder you can make a record, called a *macro*, of any often-used mouse movements or key sequences. Then you can play the macro back later with a single keystroke.

To run Recorder:

1. Open the Accessories program group.

2. Double-click on the Recorder icon. Or, use the direction keys to highlight Recorder and press ↵. The Recorder window will appear.

Notes   When you start the macro Recorder, the workspace will be empty. When you have some macros recorded and saved to disk, you can use the Open command on the File pull-down menu to load the file that contains the list of macros and select the macro you wish to use from the list.

CHANGING THE RECORDER'S OPTIONS

Recorder has four options, located in the Options menu, that control how it executes. The first three of these are toggles. Click on them to switch between active (the default) and inactive states. (A check mark appears beside a toggle menu option when it's active.) The fourth option involves a dialog box.

Control-Break Checking—allows Recorder to detect a Ctrl-Break key sequence, which interrupts macro execution. Disable this option to prevent the user from interrupting a macro.

Shortcut Keys—allows Recorder to detect shortcut keys. Disable this option if an active macro uses a shortcut key that is also used by a currently executing program.

Minimize on Use—reduces the Recorder to an icon when a macro is played.

Preferences—invokes the Default Preferences dialog box, which lets you change the default settings for Recorder. The settings you can adjust are:

- In the Playback area (Alt-P), the To drop-down list setting determines whether a macro plays only in the application in which it was recorded, or in any application

- In the Playback area (Alt-P), the Speed drop-down list setting determines the speed at which the macro replays

- The Record Mouse (Alt-M) drop-down list contains options for the type of mouse movements recorded

- The Relative To (Alt-R) drop-down list setting determines whether a macro is recorded relative to the screen or to a window

To select an option:

1. Pull down the Options menu (Alt-O) and select the desired option. If you select one of the three toggle options, a check mark will either appear or disappear, depending on whether you toggle on or off. If you select Preferences, the Default Preferences dialog box will appear. Change one or more default settings in the dialog box, as desired.

2. Click on OK or press ↵.

CHANGING A MACRO'S PROPERTIES

A macro's properties are those features that govern how the macro executes. If you record a macro, attempt to execute it, and get an error message, changing its properties may allow it to execute successfully. (See "Options," below.)

Start by making sure the Recorder is on-screen and that the macro whose properties you wish to change is listed in the Recorder workspace.

1. Click on the macro name or use the direction keys to select the macro from the listing in the Recorder workspace.

2. Pull down the Macro menu (Alt-M) and select Properties (P). The Macro Properties dialog box will appear.

3. Change any of the properties (see "Options," below).

4. Click on OK or press ↵.

5. Save the current macro file to make the changes permanent.

Options   The properties you can change are:

Macro Name (Alt-N)—the name originally assigned to the macro.

Shortcut Key (Alt-K)—the macro's shortcut key assignment. Select the key to use from the drop-down list, and choose any combination of the Ctrl, Alt, and Shift keys by enabling the desired check box.

Playback (Alt-P)—in the To drop-down list, selects whether the macro plays back only in the application in which it was recorded or in any Windows program. In the Speed drop-down list, selects the speed at which the macro plays back. Enable the Continuous Loop check box if you want the macro to play back continuously, and the Enable Shortcut Keys check box if the macro may contain shortcut keys that invoke other macros.

Description (Alt-D)—an explanation of the macro's purpose.

The only assigned setting you cannot change is Mouse Coordinates Relative To.

CREATING A NEW FILE

A new macro file can be started in two ways. You can start Recorder, create your macros in the empty window, and save them in a new file. Or, when you have a macro file loaded, you can start a new macro file by using the New command in the File pull-down menu.

DELETING A MACRO

You can permanently remove a macro from the list in a macro file. This may be necessary if you are merging two files that contain the same macro or if you no longer need a recorded macro that is in one of your macro files.

1. Click File (Alt-F) and select Open (O) to open the macro file that contains the recorded macro. The Open dialog box appears.

2. Double-click on the macro file name in the file name list (use the scroll arrows if necessary). Or, press Tab and use the direction keys to highlight the macro file name, and then press ↵.

3. Click on the macro name in the list, or use the direction keys to highlight the macro name.

4. Click Macro (Alt-M) and select Delete (D). The Recorder message box appears, asking you to confirm the deletion of the macro.

5. Click OK or press ↵. The macro is removed from the list.

6. Click File (Alt-F) and select Save (S) to save the macro file.

LOADING A MACRO FILE FROM DISK

Before you can use any macros that have been saved to disk, you must load the file containing the macro into the Recorder.

1. Run Recorder by opening the Accessories program group and double-clicking on the Recorder icon. Or, use the direction keys to highlight Recorder and press ↵. The Recorder window will appear.

2. Pull down the File menu (Alt-F) and select Open (O). The Open dialog box will appear, showing the names of the available macro files in the File Name (Alt-N) list box.

3. Double-click on the name of the macro file you wish to load, or type the file name in the File Name text box, then click on OK or press ↵.

MERGING MACRO FILES

Only one macro file can be loaded at a time in Recorder. When you have created several macro files, you may find it helpful to combine files. You can assign a new file name to your merged files, or you can save the merged files to the originally opened file.

1. Click File (Alt-F) and select Open (O) to open a Recorder file on the File Name list. Or, you can create a new file to merge into an existing file.

2. Click File again and select Merge (M). The Merge dialog box appears.

3. Double-click on the Recorder file you want to merge into your open file. Or, press Tab and use the direction keys to highlight a file in the File Name list, then press ⏎. The two files merge immediately, and the macros appear on the list in the Recorder window.

4. If you attempt to merge files containing macros that use the same shortcut key sequence, a message box appears to inform you that the duplicate key sequence has been removed and you must specify new shortcut keys for the newly merged macro. Click OK or press ⏎ to remove the message box.

5. To save the merged file with the originally opened file's name, pull down the File menu and select Save (S). To save the merged file with a new name, pull down the File menu and select Save As (A). Type a new file name in the File Name text box. The .REC extension will be added to the file name automatically.

Notes   If there is no name assigned to a macro whose shortcut key sequence was duplicated, it will appear on the macro list with the message that the shortcut keys were cleared by the merge.

RECORDING A MACRO

At the beginning of the macro recording process, you assign each macro a name and a shortcut key. The macro name can be up to 40 characters long. The shortcut key is the key sequence that will invoke the macro you record. A shortcut key is always some combination of Ctrl, Shift, Alt, and any other key. Some sample shortcut keys are Ctrl-Backspace and Shift-Alt-T.

Although Windows Recorder will allow you to create macros based
on the Alt key (Alt-F1, Alt-PgDn, etc.), it's not a good idea to do so,
since Windows has its own set of shortcut keys based on the Alt key
(to access pull-down menus, for example). If you create macros based
on the Alt key, they may interfere with Windows' functioning.

To record a macro for use within an application:

1. Run Recorder and minimize it.

2. Run the application in which the macro will operate, and
    position the cursor at exactly the point where the macro
    will begin.

3. Restore the Recorder icon to a window by double-clicking
    on it, or by pressing Alt-Tab until the Recorder program is
    listed and then releasing the Alt-Tab key combination.

4. Click on Macro (Alt-M) and select Record (C). You will see
    the screen depicted in Figure II.10. (See "Options," below.)

5. Type a name for the macro in the Record Macro Name (Alt-
    N) text box. Or, enable the Shift, Alt, and/or Ctrl check
    boxes to make the macro key sequence begin with the
    specified keystroke(s). By default, the Ctrl check box is
    enabled. If all three check boxes are enabled, the macro
    will begin with the Ctrl-Shift-Alt key sequence.

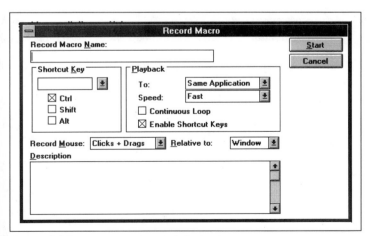

Figure II.10: The Record Macro dialog box

6. If you are assigning a shortcut key sequence, click on the Shortcut Key (Alt-K) text box and type in an alphanumeric key. Or, click on the arrow button or press Alt-↓ to reveal the drop-down list of nonalphanumeric keys. Click on the key from the list (use the scroll arrows if necessary) or use the direction keys to highlight the key and press Alt-↑.

7. Click on the Start (Alt-S) command button. Recorder will become minimized, its icon will start blinking, and the application in which the macro is to execute will become active.

8. Perform the keystrokes and mouse movements you wish to record.

9. When you are finished, click on the Recorder icon. If the application you are in is maximized, press Ctrl-Break. The Recorder dialog box will appear. Click on the option button, or use the key sequence to choose Save Macro (Alt-S), Resume Recording (Alt-R), or Cancel Recording (Alt-C).

10. Select Save Macro, then click OK or press ⏎.

Options

Record Macro Name (Alt-N)—type a descriptive name up to 40 characters long for your macro. This is required if you do not assign a shortcut key sequence to your macro.

Shortcut Key (Alt-K)—enable the Ctrl, Alt, and/or Shift options for the key(s) to begin your shortcut key sequence. (Ctrl is enabled by default.) Type an alphanumeric key in the text box, or select a nonalphanumeric key from the drop-down list. A shortcut key sequence is required if you do not name your macro.

Playback (Alt-P)—the Playback area of the Record Macro dialog box contains the settings for running the macro.

> **To**—play back the macro only in the application in which it was recorded, or play the macro in any application.
>
> **Speed**—run the macro at fast speed, or at the speed at which it was recorded.
>
> **Continuous Loop**—run the macro continuously.

Enable Shortcut Keys—allows "nesting" of macros (the default). As many as five macros can be combined into one macro.

Record Mouse (Alt-M)—select from the drop-down list whether to record mouse movements.

Clicks & Drags—records keystrokes and all mouse movements as long as a mouse button is pressed (the default).

Ignore Mouse—no mouse movements are recorded, only keystrokes. This option should be selected when preparing a macro for use by different people who work on different machines. Mouse movements will not function correctly unless the video adapter where the macro is run is exactly like the one where the macro was recorded.

Everything—records all mouse movements and keystrokes.

Relative To (Alt-R)—records a macro relative to the window (the default) or to the entire screen. The option selected when recording a macro cannot be modified using the Macro Properties dialog box.

Description (Alt-D)—allows you to type an explanation for your macro longer than the 40 characters allowed in the Record Macro Name text box.

Notes You must assign either a Shortcut Key or a Macro Name to your macro. It is advisable to assign both, especially if you intend to merge your macro files. Many macros can be stored in one macro file.

You do not need to change other options in the Record Macros dialog box unless you are recording a more complex macro.

When recording a macro, use as few mouse movements as possible. Use keystrokes whenever possible so the macro can be played back in a window of a different size.

If you are recording all mouse movements, use the Ctrl-Break key sequence to stop macro recording. Otherwise, your mouse movements to stop the recording will also be recorded and the macro may play back with unexpected results.

RUNNING A MACRO

To run a macro is to enact a previously recorded series of keystrokes and/or mouse movements. Your keyboard and mouse are temporarily turned off while the macro executes. (You can interrupt the macro by pressing Ctrl-Break.)

To run a macro, Windows Recorder must be active and the desired macro must be loaded into the program. This involves using a macro that was just created, or loading a previously recorded macro from disk (see "Loading a Macro File from Disk").

To play back a macro that was recorded for a specific application:

1. Minimize the Recorder window.

2. Open the application and place the cursor where the macro will play back.

3. Press the shortcut key sequence assigned to the macro.

To play back a macro that was recorded beginning with an unopened application:

- With the Recorder window open, double-click on the macro in the list or press the macro's shortcut key sequence. Or, using the direction keys, select the macro in the list, click Macro (Alt-M), and select Run (R). The macro will execute.

Notes If you have not assigned a shortcut key sequence to the macro, you must use the Run command from the Macro pull-down menu. If the macro is not started exactly at the point where recording began, an error message will appear and the macro will not execute.

SAVING A MACRO FILE

Macros can be saved to disk and reused at a later time. Before you can save a set of macros, the macros must be recorded and listed in the Recorder workspace. Macro files in which you have added, deleted, or modified macros must be saved in order to save your changes. Macro disk files end in an .REC extension. See "Saving Files" for the standard saving procedure.

MICROSOFT WRITE

Write is a word processing program from Microsoft that works within the Windows environment. Its icon is in the Accessories program group. Write performs all necessary word processing functions, such as block copying, moving, and deleting. It creates and manipulates italic, superscript, subscript, boldfaced, and underlined text. Write also has an undo function, and can find text within a document and replace it with whatever text you designate. In Windows 3.1, Write also supports object linking and embedding (OLE).

1. Open the Accessories program group.

2. Double-click on the Write icon, or use the direction keys to highlight Write and then press ↵. The Write window will appear.

EDITING AND FORMATTING IN WRITE

Cutting, Copying, and Pasting Text

Like almost every other Windows program, Write will allow you to select information and copy it into a reserved portion of memory called the Clipboard. You can delete the selected text from the document as you place it in the Clipboard, which is called *cutting,* or you can simply copy it. Text placed in the Clipboard can be copied back into the current document at any point you specify. This is called *pasting.* The text can also be pasted into any other application running under Windows that will accept textual data.

1. Select the text you wish to cut or copy to the Clipboard. (See "Selecting Text.")

2. Click Edit (Alt-E) and select either Cut (T) or Copy (C). Or, press Ctrl-X to cut or Ctrl-C to copy the text. The selected text is now in the Clipboard.

3. Place the cursor where you want the text to appear in your current document or in another document.

4. Pull down the Edit menu again and select Paste (P). Or, press Ctrl-V to paste the text at the cursor location.

See Also Pasting Data from the Clipboard

Displaying and Hiding the Ruler

The Ruler, a graphic image of a ruler Write places at the top of the document window, helps you determine exactly where text is placed on the page (see Figure II.11). If you are using a mouse, it also lets you easily set tabs, indents, line spacing, and justification. To toggle the Ruler on and off, start with the Write window on-screen.

- Click on Document (Alt-D) and toggle Ruler On or Ruler Off (R).

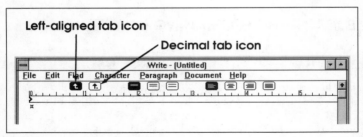

Figure II.11: The Ruler

Formatting Characters

Changing Fonts and Font Sizes

In Windows usage, a font is a graphically rendered image of a particular typeface. Fonts are named after the typefaces they represent—Courier, Times Roman, Helvetica, etc. The default font for Write is Arial (a TrueType font), set at 10 characters per inch (CPI). You can change fonts at any time and use any of the fonts installed in the Windows environment.

To change the font using the Fonts command:

1. Place the cursor at the location where you want the new font to start, or select the text to which you want to assign a new font.

2. Click Character (Alt-C) and then click Fonts (F). The Font dialog box appears.

3. In the Font (Alt-F) list box, click on the name of the new font you wish to appear in the Write window (use the scroll arrows if necessary), or use the direction keys to highlight a new font name. Each time a new font is selected, the font style and size options also change.

4. In the Font Style (Alt-Y) list box, click on the style or use the direction keys to highlight the style you wish to appear in the directory window.

5. In the Size (Alt-S) list box, select a new size by clicking on a size (use the scroll arrows if necessary) or using the direction keys to highlight it.

6. When you have made all the desired changes, click OK or press ↵.

To change the font size using the Character menu:

1. Place the cursor at the location where you want the new font size to start, or select the text to which you want to assign a new font size.

2. Click Character (Alt-C) and then select Reduce Font (R) or Enlarge Font (E). The font size of the text will change as specified.

Notes Each time a selection is made in the Font, Font Style, or Size list box, an example of the selection is shown in the Sample area of the Font dialog box.

When the Reduce Font or Enlarge Font command is selected, the specified text is sized in the next smaller or larger font size. If your default printer does not support the selected size, the text will not appear resized on the screen.

Changing the Text Style

The term "text style" refers to the appearance of text both on the
screen and on the printed page. Write will format text in several
styles: underlined, boldfaced, and italic.

1. Place the cursor at the location where you want to start
   typing in the new style, or select the text whose style you
   want to change.

2. Click Character (Alt-C) and select Bold (B), Italic (I),
   and/or Underline (U) as the text style. Or, press one of the
   following key combinations:

   • For Bold, press Ctrl-B
   • For Italic, press Ctrl-I
   • For Underline, press Ctrl-U

Write also allows you to add superscript or subscript formatting to
text. Superscript is text that appears somewhat above other text;
subscript is text that appears somewhat below. Both superscript
and subscript appear in a smaller size than the surrounding text.

1. Place the cursor at the location where you want to start
   typing in the new style, or select the text whose style you
   want to change.

2. Click Character (Alt-C) and select Superscript (P) or Subscript (C) as the text style.

Notes   Bold, italic, and underline text styles can be chosen in any
combination. Superscript or subscript are mutually exclusive: you
can choose one or the other. You can use superscript or subscript in
combination with bold, italic, and/or underlined text.

Removing a Text Style

You can cancel any or all of your selected text styles with one
command.

1. Place the cursor at the location where you want to cancel
   the selected style(s), or select the text whose style you
   want to remove.

2. Click Character (Alt-C) and select Regular (G). Or, press the F5 key. All formatting is removed from the text.

Formatting a Document

Write commands allow you to change the default format for the entire document. You can add headers and/or footers, change the margins, or select inches or centimeters as the measurement setting.

Adding Headers and/or Footers

A Write document can contain one header and one footer. A header is a line of text that appears above the top margin on each page of the document. A footer is a line of text that appears below the bottom margin of each page in the document.

Write commands allow you to begin the header or footer on either the first or the second page of the document, enter the line of text, specify a new measurement for the location of the header and/or footer, and print the page number. The header and footer do not appear in the document window; they only appear on the printed document.

1. Click Document (Alt-D) and select Header (H) or Footer (F). The Page Header or Page Footer dialog box appears inside the Header window or the Footer window.

2. In the Header or Footer window, type the text you wish to appear on your printed page.

3. Click in the Page Header or the Page Footer dialog box to activate it, or press Alt-F6.

4. If necessary, type a new measurement in the Distance from Top or Distance from Bottom (both use the Alt-D key sequence) text box.

5. To print the header or footer on the first page of the document, enable the Print on First Page (Alt-P) option. The default is disabled, which means the header or footer will begin to print on the second page of the document.

6. If you want the page number to appear in the header or footer, click the Insert Page # command button or press

Alt-I. The page number will be added at the location of the insertion point in the Header or Footer window.

7. When you have entered all the information for your header or footer, click Return to Document (Alt-R).

Notes   The text in the Header or Footer window can be formatted using the same options as the text in a document. If you make a mistake while typing your text, you can use the Write Edit commands or the Backspace key to perform your edits, or, in the Page Header or Page Footer dialog box, select the Clear (Alt-C) command button to remove all the text in the window.

Choosing the Starting Page Number

When the first page of your document is a cover page, you may need to start with a page number other than 1. The number entered in the Page Layout dialog box determines what page number is displayed on the Write window status line, and also the page used in the Go To command.

To change the starting page number:

1. Click Document (Alt-D) and select Page Layout (P). The Page Layout dialog box appears.

2. Type the new page number in the Start Page Numbers At (Alt-S) text box.

3. Click OK or press ⏎ to accept the new starting page number.

Inserting a Page Break

Write treats your document as one page on-screen until you add page breaks. If you want to see what will be on each page before the document is printed, you must add the page breaks either automatically or manually.

To add page breaks automatically:

1. Click File (Alt-F) and select Repaginate (E). The Repaginate Document dialog box appears.

2. If you want to review each page break as it is made, enable the Confirm Page Breaks (Alt-B) option.

3. Click OK or press ↵ to create the document page breaks. The automatic page breaks are indicated by two small arrows to the left of the first line on the new page.

To add page breaks manually:

1. Move the insertion point to the position where you wish to place the page break.

2. Press Ctrl-↵. The manual page break is indicated by a dotted line in the document.

If you enabled the Confirm Page Breaks option, the Repaginating Document dialog box appears:

- When an automatic page break is encountered, you have the option of moving the page break Up (Alt-U), you can Confirm (Alt-C) the page break, or you can Cancel (press Tab until Cancel is highlighted and then press ↵) the repagination. The Down (Alt-D) command button can be used only if you have previously moved the page break up.

- When a manual page break is encountered, you may Keep (Alt-K) the page break, Remove (Alt-R) it, or Cancel the repagination.

Notes   Automatic page breaks cannot be removed. Manually inserted page breaks can be removed.

Setting Margins

Margins are the boundaries of the printed page. The left and right margins are the distances between the text and the left and right edges of the page, respectively. The top margin is the distance between the first line of text and the top of the page, and the bottom margin is the distance between the baseline of the text and the bottom of the page. Write allows you to change all of these margins.

1. Click on Document (Alt-D) and select Page Layout (P). The Page Layout dialog box appears.

2. In the Margins area, click and drag on the text box for the margin you wish to change to highlight the current margin setting. Or, use the key sequence (Alt-L for left, Alt-R

for right, Alt-T for Top, and Alt-B for the bottom margin)
to highlight the appropriate text box. Type in the new margin setting.

3. Click OK or press ↵ to reset the margins.

Formatting a Paragraph

The default format in Write is single-spaced, left-aligned, no indent
for paragraphs. You can change the line spacing, paragraph alignment, and indentation of a single paragraph or of selected paragraphs. Each new paragraph has the same formatting as the
preceding paragraph.

To format a single paragraph, move the insertion point anywhere in
the paragraph and specify the paragraph settings. To format
several paragraphs at once, select text in adjacent paragraphs
before specifying the settings. To format all paragraphs in a document the same way, specify the paragraph settings before you
begin typing.

To Use the Paragraph Menu

1. With the Write window open, click Paragraph (Alt-P) and
   toggle the options for paragraph alignment and line spacing. (See "Options," below.)

2. To indent the paragraph(s), pull down the Paragraph
   menu again and select Indents (I). The Indents dialog box
   will appear.

3. Type the measurement for Left Indent (Alt-L), First Line
   (Alt-F), and/or Right Indent (Alt-R) in the text box. The
   measurement will be in inches or centimeters, depending
   on the setting selected in the Page Layout dialog box.

4. Click OK or press ↵ to set the paragraph indents.

Options

Normal (N)—returns the paragraph to single-spaced, left-jus-
tified format and removes all indentation.

Left (L)—aligns graphics and text along the left margin.

Centered (C)—aligns graphics and text in the center between both the left and the right margins.

Right (R)—aligns text and graphics along the right margin.

Justified (J)—aligns text evenly along both the left and the right margins.

Single Space (S)—sets line spacing to single-spaced.

1 ½ Space (1) —sets line spacing to 1½ lines.

Double Space (D)—sets line spacing to double-spaced.

Indents (I)—sets indentation for the entire paragraph and/or the first line of the paragraph.

> **Left Indent (Alt-L)**—type a measurement in the text box to indent the entire paragraph aligned along the left margin.

> **First Line (Alt-F)**—the specified measurement indents only the first line of the paragraph aligned along the left margin.

> **Right Indent (Alt-R)**—the measurement specified indents the entire paragraph aligned along the right margin.

To Use the Ruler

The Ruler provides a graphic representation of the selected paragraph formatting. The line-spacing icon, paragraph alignment icon, and the icons for left indent, right indent, and first-line indent reflect the setting for the paragraph that holds the insertion point.

If you are using a mouse, you can set the line spacing, paragraph alignment, and indentation with the Ruler displayed and the insertion point in the paragraph you wish to change.

To set the line spacing or paragraph alignment:

- Click on one of the three line-spacing icons to select line spacing for the paragraph. The icons represent single-spacing, 1½-line spacing, and double-spacing.

- Click on one of the four paragraph alignment icons to select the paragraph alignment. The icons represent left, centered, right, and justified text alignment.

To set the indentation:

- Click and drag the first-line, left, or right indent icon along the bottom of the Ruler to the desired location.

Moving and Editing Keys

To move within a Write document and perform editing functions, you can use many different key sequences. You can use key sequences to move the cursor to the beginning or the end of the document, and to the top or bottom of a window. Table II.1 lists key sequences for moving in a Write document.

Other key sequences allow you to cut, copy, or paste text or graphics. Table II.2 lists these key sequences for editing in a Write document.

Searching

You can search for one or several characters or words in a Write document and, if you wish, edit the characters found.

1. With the insertion point positioned where the search should begin in the document, click Find (Alt-N) and select Find (F). The Find dialog box appears.

2. Type the text you want to search for in the Find What (Alt-N) text box. You can use wildcard characters (see "Options," below).

3. If you want to search for the specified text as a whole word, click on the check box or press Alt-W to enable the Match Whole Word Only option.

4. If you want to search for the specified text with exactly the same upper- and lowercase letters, click on the check box or press Alt-C to enable the Match Case option.

5. Click Find Next (Alt-F) to search for the first occurrence of the specified text.

Table II.1: Cursor Movement in Column Mode

To Go To	Use This Key Sequence
Previous sentence	5-←
Next sentence	5-→
Previous paragraph	5-↑
Next paragraph	5-↓
Previous page	5-Page Up
Next page	5-Page Down
Previous word	Ctrl-←
Next word	Ctrl-→
Beginning of line	Home
End of line	End
Top of window	Ctrl-Page Up
Bottom of window	Ctrl-Page Down
Beginning of document	Ctrl-Home
End of document	Ctrl-End

6. If necessary, you can edit the found text by clicking on the document where you wish to place the insertion point, or pressing Alt-F6 to select the specified text and activate the document. To return to the Find dialog box, click on the dialog box or press Alt-F6 again.

7. Repeat step 5 until you have finished searching for the text. You may need to move the Find dialog box to reveal found text. (See "Moving Windows and Icons.")

8. A message box appears to inform you that Write cannot find any more instances of the specified text. Click OK or press ↵.

9. When you have finished your search, click Cancel or press Esc to remove the Find dialog box.

Table II.2: Key Sequences for Editing in Write

Action	Key Sequence
Insert a manual page break	Ctrl-↵
Cut text to the Clipboard	Ctrl-X
Copy text to the Clipboard	Ctrl-C
Paste text to the Clipboard	Ctrl-V
Undo last edit	Ctrl-Z
Delete selected text	Delete
Insert optional hyphen	Ctrl-Shift-Hyphen
Select a graphic	↓
Resize a graphic	Arrow Key
Select between window and dialog box	Alt-F6
Repeat last find	F3
Go to page	F4
Regular text format	F5
Bold	Ctrl-B
Italics	Ctrl-I
Underline	Ctrl-U

Options

Type a question mark (?) to represent one character in the specified text.

Type ^w to search for any space in the document.

Type ^t to search for a tab.

Type ^P to find paragraph marks.

Type ^d to find manual page breaks.

Replacing Characters

Using the Replace command, you can find specified text and replace it with new text. You have the option of replacing individual occurrences or all instances of the specified text, and you can select a portion of text on which to perform the search and replace operations.

1. With the insertion point positioned where the search should begin in the document, or a portion of the text selected, click Find (Alt-N) and select Replace (E). The Replace dialog box appears.

2. Type the text you want to search for in the Find What (Alt-N) text box. You can use wildcard characters (see "Options" under "Searching").

3. If you want to search for the specified text as a whole word, click on the check box or press Alt-W to enable the Match Whole Word Only option.

4. If you want to search for the specified text with exactly the same upper- and lowercase letters, click on the check box or press Alt-C to enable the Match Case option.

5. Click Find Next (Alt-F) to search for the first occurrence of the specified text. If you wish to replace it with the new text, click Replace (Alt-R). If you do not want to replace the text, select Find Next again to continue the search. Repeat this step until you have completed your search and replace operation.

6. If you want to replace each occurrence of the text in the document, click Replace All (Alt-A). If you have selected a portion of the text in which to conduct the search and replace operation, click Replace Selection (Alt-S).

7. When you have completed your search and replace operation, click Close or press Alt-L to remove the Replace dialog box.

Notes   A message box informs you when Write cannot find any occurrences of the specified text. Click OK or press ↵ to remove the message box.

The search for specified text begins at the location of the insertion point. When the search comes to the end of the document, it resumes at the beginning of the document until the insertion point is reached again.

The Match Whole Word Only and the Match Case options can both be selected at the same time to find an exact match of the desired text.

Selecting Text

Write allows you to select portions of text in several ways. Text must be selected before you can change its font style, underline it, or boldface it. You must also select text in order to cut or copy it to the Clipboard.

Start with the text you wish to select visible in the Write window.

1. Using the mouse or direction keys, place the cursor at the beginning of the text you wish to select.

2. Click and hold down the left mouse button, or press and hold down the Shift key.

3. Drag the pointer to the lower-right corner of the text, or use the direction keys to highlight the desired text.

4. Release the mouse button or the Shift key. The text is now selected.

If you are using a mouse, you can also select text by using a portion of the screen called the *selection area*. The selection area is an invisible vertical line on the left side of the Write workspace; the pointer slants to the right when it is in the selection area.

With the mouse pointer in the selection area, use the following procedures for selecting text:

- One line—Click on the line
- Multiple lines—Click on a line and drag the mouse pointer up or down. Release the mouse button when the desired text is highlighted
- One paragraph—Double-click on the paragraph
- Multiple paragraphs—Double-click to select the paragraph, then, while holding the second mouse click, drag the mouse pointer up or down to select additional paragraphs

- A text range—Click to select the first line or double-click to select the first paragraph. Then move the mouse pointer to the ending paragraph or line and, while pressing the Shift key, click the mouse button. The text between the first and the last line or paragraph is selected

- The whole document—Click the mouse button while holding down the Ctrl key

See Also   Changing Fonts and Font Sizes; Changing the Text Style; Cutting, Copying, and Pasting Text

Setting Tabs

Write's tabs are preset at one-half inch. Using the Tabs command or the Ruler, you can override these tabs and set up to 12 tabs of your own. You can set either regular or decimal tabs. (A decimal tab aligns typed numbers on their decimal points.)

To Use the Tabs Command

1. Click Document (Alt-D) and select Tabs (T). The Tabs dialog box will appear.

2. Type a measurement in the first available Positions (Alt-P) text box. The measurement will represent the distance from the left margin to the tab.

3. If you are creating a decimal tab, click on the Decimal (Alt-D) check box below the Positions text box you selected in step 2.

4. Repeat steps 2–3 as needed.

5. Click OK or press ↵ to activate the new tab positions. The newly created tab positions appear on the Ruler (if it is displayed).

To Use the Ruler

If you are using a mouse, Write offers an easy and intuitive way to set tabs with the Ruler. The Ruler uses tab icons and tab markers to help you create tabs and to indicate their location (see Figure II.11).

1. Make sure the Ruler is visible (see "Displaying and Hiding the Ruler").

2. Select the type of tab you wish to set. The icon appears in reverse video.

3. Place the mouse pointer over the point on the Ruler line where you want the tab, and click. A tab marker will appear. Be careful not to click on the Ruler's graduations, as this won't produce the desired effect.

Undoing Your Last Edit

Write allows you to undo the last edit you made to a document, using the Undo command. You can return deleted data, replace new text formatting with the original, or remove the last data entered. Both text and graphics errors can be "undone." The Undo command changes, depending on the last action you performed.

*   As soon as you decide to return to your original text or format, or to replace your original text, click Edit (Alt-E) and click Undo Typing, Undo Formatting, or Undo Editing (whichever option is displayed) or press U. Or, press Ctrl-Z, the undo key sequence. The typing, editing, or formatting is removed.

*   To restore the just-removed text, formatting, or an edit, select Edit again and select Undo (U). Or, press Ctrl-Z again.

GRAPHICS

You can insert or, in Windows 3.1, embed a graphic in a Windows Write document. The graphic can be moved or resized according to your needs. An embedded graphic can be edited from within the Write document; to embed or edit an embedded graphic, see the instructions in the the Appendix.

Inserting a Graphic

You can insert or paste graphics from other programs into Write documents. This is accomplished using the Clipboard. When a graphic is inserted into Write, it is automatically aligned with the left margin. Its resolution will match that of the default printer, not the video display.

Start with the Write document opened on the desktop, and the source application active.

1. Cut or copy the desired graphic into the Windows Clipboard (see "Copying or Cutting Data into the Clipboard").

2. Switch back to Write.

3. Place the mouse pointer at the vertical location where you want the graphic to appear.

4. Click on Edit (Alt-E) and select Paste (P). Or, press Ctrl-V. The graphic will appear in the Write document.

Moving a Graphic

Write allows you to move a graphic horizontally in a document. You can select the graphic and reposition it using the Paragraph formatting commands (Left, Centered, or Right), or you can use the mouse or the direction keys to place the graphic where you wish.

1. Click on the graphic or use the ↑ and ↓ keys to select it. The graphic will appear in inverse colors.

2. Click Edit (Alt-E) and select Move Picture (M). The mouse pointer will change into a picture of a box in the middle of the graphic. The graphic will be surrounded by a rectangle.

3. Drag the mouse or use the ← and → keys to move the rectangle to the desired location.

4. Click the left mouse button or press ↵.

Sizing a Graphic

Write allows you to adjust the size of a graphic so that you can create correctly formatted documents. When you size a graphic, you can change its width by adjusting the left or right border of the image and its length by pulling down the lower border. You cannot adjust the upper border.

1. Select the graphic by clicking on it or using the direction keys. The graphic will appear in inverse colors.

2. Pull down the Edit menu (Alt-E) and select Size Picture (S). The mouse pointer changes into a picture of a box and moves to the center of the image. The graphic will be surrounded by a rectangle.

3. Drag the pointer to the left, right, or down, and the corresponding border will be selected. (You can do the same thing using the ←, →,or ↓ keys.) You can then reposition the selected border. If you wish to size the image diagonally, select two borders at once—the right and bottom borders, for example.

4. If your graphic is not sized as you wish, press Esc and repeat steps 2–3.

5. Click the left mouse button or press ↵.

LINKING OR EMBEDDING AN OBJECT

Windows 3.1 allows Paintbrush, Sound Recorder, and Object Packager to link or embed objects in a document file. See the Appendix for information on how to link or embed an object in a Write document, and how to edit the objects.

OPENING A FILE IN WRITE

Opening a document in Microsoft Write consists of reading the file contents from the disk and loading them into Write. You can open Write files (files with a .WRI extension) or Windows text files, which are files in ANSI format. You can also open Microsoft Word files in the Write window.

Start with the Write window on-screen.

Opening a Windows Text File or a Word Document

Follow the instructions given in "Opening a File" under "Standard Operations." The Write conversion message box will appear. If the selected file is a Windows text file, click No Conversion or press Alt-N. If the file is a Microsoft Word file, click Convert or press ↵. The file will open in the Write window.

Opening a Write Document

See "Opening a File" under "Standard Operations."

Opening a New Document

Write will allow you to start a new document if you have already opened a file. You will be prompted to save any changes to the currently open file.

- Click File (Alt-F) and select New (N). The contents of the Write window will be replaced with a blank document.

Notes   Only one document at a time can be open in Write. A message box appears if you have changed the open document and attempted to open another document. You can choose to save your changes to the file, or lose the changes by not saving the document to file. You can also cancel the attempt in order to save your currently open file to a new file name. (See "Saving a Write Document.")

PRINTING AN OPEN DOCUMENT

The document that is currently open in Write can be printed to either the printer or a file. See "Setting Up the Printer" under "Standard Operations."

Changing Printers

If you have installed more than one printer, you may select a
printer other than the default to print your Write document. You
can also change some of the printer options such as the size of the
paper, the page orientation, and the paper source. Each printer driver
has its own unique options, so not all options are available for all
printers. See "Changing Printers" under "Standard Operations"

SAVING A WRITE DOCUMENT

Write will save any document you edit to a disk file. To save a document, start with the Write window open and the text you wish to
save on-screen. Follow the instructions given in "Saving Files"
under "Standard Operations."

Saving in a Different Format

You can also choose to have Write save your document in any of
these formats:

Write 3.0 (.WRI)—appears in the list only when an object has
been linked or embedded in the file. The embedded or linked
object is removed from the file so the file can be used in Windows 3.0. (See the Appendix for information on linked and embedded objects.)

Word for DOS (.DOC)—Microsoft Word format. All formatting and graphics will be lost.

Word for DOS/Txt Only (.DOC)—Microsoft Word text file
with no formatting.

Text Files (.TXT)—standard ASCII format with paragraph
breaks, but no line breaks or graphics.

All Files—saves the document to any file name, but with Write
format.

Note that Write will save documents in Word for DOS format, but not in Word for Windows format. Word for Windows will allow you to convert Write files when they are opened.

1. Save the current document.

2. Click on File (Alt-F) and select Save As (A). The Save As dialog box appears.

3. Type the file name in the File Name (Alt-N) text box, but omit the file extension.

4. Click the arrow button, or press Alt-T and then press Alt-↓ to reveal the Save File as Type drop-down list. Click on the file type, or use the direction keys to highlight the file type and press Alt-↑.

5. Click OK or press ↵. The file will be saved with the specified file type extension.

Notes   When Write saves a document to the Microsoft Word format, it automatically assigns the file a .DOC extension. When it saves to the ASCII format, it automatically assigns the .TXT extension.

Backing Up Your Files

You can make an automatic backup of your Write file each time you resave it.

•   The first time you save the file, click on the Backup check box or press Alt-B in the File Save As Dialog box.

Notes   When you save a Write file in Write format, the .BKP extension is assigned to the file. When the file is saved in Microsoft Word format, the backup file is given the .BAK extension. If you change the .WRI extension of a Write file to save it as a Microsoft Word file, the backup file becomes the original .WRI file. If you change the .DOC extension of a Microsoft Word file to a save it as a Write file, the backup file becomes the original .DOC file.

NOTEPAD OPERATIONS

Notepad, a Windows application whose icon is in the Accessories program group, is an ASCII (American Standard Code for Information Interchange) text editor. Notepad is useful for writing quick notes and memos. You can also use Notepad to create and edit batch files, or to edit the system configuration files, CONFIG.SYS and AUTOEXEC.BAT. Notepad offers only rudimentary word processing features, such as word wrap and the ability to search for any text you specify. It does not format characters, paragraphs, or documents.

CREATING A NOTE

1. Open the Accessories program group.

2. Double-click on the Notepad icon, or use the direction keys to highlight Notepad and press ↵. The Notepad window will appear.

3. To create a note, start typing. When you reach the right side of the window, the text will disappear off the edge as you type. To make the text automatically move to the next line, set Notepad's word wrap feature on (see "Word Wrap").

CREATING A TIME LOG

A time log is a record of the times and dates when a Notepad file was edited. Notepad will keep a time log within a file, provided you specify it as a time log file.

1. Open or create a note (see "Opening a Note" or "Creating a Note").

2. At the beginning of the first line in the file, type **.LOG**. Make sure you use uppercase letters.

3. Save the note to disk (see "Saving a Note"). Now, every time you open this file, Notepad will automatically insert the time and date at the end of the file.

CUTTING AND COPYING TEXT

Text within Notepad can be cut or copied into the Windows Clipboard, much like text in any other Windows program. You must first select the text. See "Selecting Text" and "Cutting, Copying, and Pasting Text," both under "Microsoft Write."

FINDING TEXT

Notepad can search the text of an open file and find any string of characters you specify. Using the Search (Alt-S) menu in place of the find (Alt-N) menu, follow the instructionss in "Searching" under "Microsoft Write."

INSERTING THE DATE AND TIME

At any point when you are editing a text file, Notepad can insert the date and time.

   1.   Place the cursor at exactly the point where you want the
            date and time to appear.

   2.   Click on Edit (Alt-E) and select Time/Date (D), or press F5.

OPENING A NOTE

To open a file is to read it from the disk into Notepad. By default, Notepad files have a .TXT extension. You can assign any extension you wish to a Notepad file (i.e., .BAT or .SYS). Notepad file are opened in the standard manner; see "Opening a File" under "Standard Operations."

To create a new note when you have a note already open, open a blank window by clicking File (Alt-F) and selecting New (N).

PRINTING A DOCUMENT

Printing a document from Notepad is a very simple procedure. Once you've selected the Print option, Notepad will immediately send the entire document to the Print Manager. You will not be given the option of printing specific pages or selected text, as you would be with more powerful text editors.

- Click on File (Alt-F) and select Print (P).

Notes Notepad gives you the option of selecting a different default printer, including headers and footers, and changing the margins. See "Setting Up a Page" and "Setting Up the Printer," both under "Standard Operations."

SAVING A NOTE

When Notepad saves a file, it saves the text in standard ASCII format and automatically assigns the .TXT file extension unless you specify a different extension. It also writes the file to the Windows directory unless you specify otherwise when you save it. Files created by Notepad are saved in the standard manner; see "Saving Files" under "Standard Operations."

WORD WRAP

Word Wrap is an option that allows Notepad to wrap text to the next line when the right border of the window is reached.

- Click Edit (Alt-E) and select Word Wrap (W). A check mark appears in front of the option. Repeat this step to toggle Word Wrap off.

OBJECT PACKAGER

The Object Packager is a Windows application that operates with object linking and embedding (OLE), a capability new in Windows 3.1. It is used to create an object (the "package"), which appears as an icon, that can be embedded in or linked to a document. The Object Packager is located in the Accessories program group.

The Object Packager window, shown in Figure II.12, contains two "panes": the Appearance pane is on the left and the Content pane is

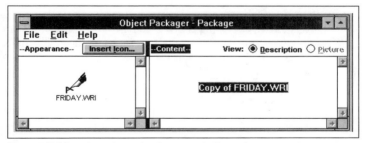

Figure II.12: The Object Packager window

on the right. The Appearance pane contains the icon that appears in a destination document to symbolize the linked or embedded object. The Content pane shows the name of the document that includes the object, or a picture of the object.

To open the Object Packager:

- Double-click on the icon in the Accessories program group window.

- Or, use the direction keys to highlight Object Packager, then press ↵.

CHANGING THE ICON

When an object is created, the default icon for the package is the icon of the program used to create the object. You can select another program's icon, select an icon included with Program Manager, or create your own icon for the package.

Start with Object Packager open and both panes empty.

Choosing a Different Icon

1. Open the document containing the icon you wish to replace.

2. Click on the icon or use the direction keys to select it. Pull down the application's Edit (Alt-E) menu and select Copy (C), or press Ctrl-C to copy the icon to the Clipboard.

3.   Switch to Object Packager, click on Edit (Alt-E), and select Paste (P). Or, press Ctrl-V to paste the Clipboard contents in the Object Packger window. The selected icon appears in the Appearance pane.

4.   Click Insert Icon (Alt-I). The Insert Icon dialog box appears.

5.   Type a new program name in the File Name (Alt-F) text box. Use the PROGMAN.EXE file to view the icons included in Program Manager. Or, click Browse (Alt-B) to open the Browse dialog box and double-click on a program name. You can also press Tab to move the cursor to the File Name list box, use the direction keys to highlight the program name, and press ↵. The program name appears in the File Name text box and the program icons appear in the Current Icon scroll box in the Insert Icon dialog box.

6.   Click OK or press ↵ to accept the new icon. It appears in the Appearance pane of the Object Packager window.

7.   Pull down the Object Packager's Edit (Alt-E) menu and select Copy Package (K).

8.   Once again, select the icon you wish to replace in the document. Pull down the application's Edit (Alt-E) menu and select Paste (P), or press Ctrl-V. The selected icon is replaced with the new icon.

Designing an Icon

1.   Follow steps 1–3, above.

2.   If the Appearance pane is not selected, click on the pane or press Tab to select it. Pull down the Edit (Alt-E) menu and select Copy (C), or press Ctrl-C to copy the icon in the Appearance pane to the Clipboard.

3.   Open Paintbrush.

4.   Pull down Paintbrush's Edit (Alt-E) menu and select Paste (P), or press Ctrl-V. The icon appears in the Paintbrush workspace.

5. You can alter the icon as you wish, or erase it and create your own design.

6. Pull down the Paintbrush File (Alt-F) menu and select Save (S) or Save As (A) to save the new icon.

7. Select the new drawing in the Paintbrush workspace. Pull down the Edit menu again and select Copy, or press Ctrl-C to copy the drawing to the Clipboard.

8. Switch back to the Object Packager, and make sure the Appearance pane is selected again.

9. Pull down the Edit menu and select Paste, or press Ctrl-V to paste the new drawing in the Appearance pane.

10. Pull down the Object Packager Edit menu again, and select Copy Package (K).

11. Switch back to the document and select the icon you wish to replace.

12. From the application's menu bar, pull down the Edit (Alt-E) menu and select Paste (P). Or, press Ctrl-V. The newly created icon appears in the document.

Notes　Use the Alt-Tab key sequence to switch among open applications. (See " The Desktop Display" under "Configuring Windows with the Control Panel.")

If you designed your own icon, it will not have a label.

When you replace an object icon in a document, you must save the document in order for the new icon to appear the next time the document is opened.

COPYING, CUTTING, OR DELETING THE WINDOW CONTENTS

When an icon is in the Appearance pane of the Object Manager, you can copy or cut the contents of either pane to the Clipboard. Delete is available as an option when either pane's contents are selected.

With an icon displayed and the Appearance pane selected:

- Click on Edit (Alt-E) and select Copy (C). Or, click on Edit (Alt-E) and select Cut (T).

Or, with the contents of either the Appearance pane or the Content pane selected:

- Click on Edit (Alt-E) and select Delete (D).

CREATING A PACKAGE

A package can be an entire document, or a part of a document. To package part of a document, you must use Object Packager and the document must be a server application document. No matter how the package was created, it can be inserted only in a client application document.

Adding a DOS Command

With Object Packager, you can package a DOS command line, embed it as an object in a document, and activate the package to execute the DOS command. This is useful if you wish to open another application or execute a batch file.

Start with Object Packager open.

1. Click on Edit (Alt-E) and select Command Line (M). The Command Line dialog box appears.

2. Type your command line, if necessary including the options or parameters, in the Command (Alt-C) text box. Include the full path and file extension if the command line is a program file you wish to execute.

3. Click OK or press ↵. The command line appears in the Content pane of the Object Packager.

4. Click Insert Icon (Alt-I). The Insert Icon dialog box appears.

5. Click the scroll buttons to select an icon from those available in the Current Icons scroll box, or press Alt-C and use the direction keys to highlight one of the icons. If no appropriate icon is available, click on the Browse button or

press Alt-B to reveal the Browse dialog box. (See "Browsing" in "Standard Operations.") Double-click on a program name. Or, press Tab, use the direction keys to highlight a program name, and then press ⌐ to select the program's icon. The icon appears in the Current Icon scroll box.

6. Click OK or press ⌐. The selected icon is displayed in the Appearance pane of the Object Packager.

7. Click on Edit (Alt-E) and select Copy Package (K).

8. Open the client document and move the insertion point to where you wish to embed the command package.

9. Pull down the Edit (Alt-E) menu of the client application and select Paste (P), or press Ctrl-V. The command package is displayed as an icon in the target document.

Notes   In some applications, the package may automatically be placed at the upper-left corner of the document, no matter where you located the insertion point.

Working with an Entire Document

An object is linked to or embedded in Object Packager when a package is created.

You can use Object Packager or File Manager to package an entire document, and the document application need not support OLE.

Creating a Package with Object Packager

1. Click on File (Alt-F) and select Import (I). The Import dialog box appears.

2. To select a new directory, double-click on the directory. Or, press Alt-D to move the cursor to the Directories list box, use the direction keys to highlight a directory, and press ⌐.

3. Double-click on the file you wish to package. Or, press Alt-N and then Tab to move the cursor to the File Name list box, use the direction keys to highlight the file name, and press ⌐. The icon of the program used to create the document is displayed in the Appearance pane, and the file name is displayed in the Content pane.

4. Click on Edit (Alt-E) and select Copy Package (K) to copy the package to the Clipboard.

5. Open the document and, if necessary, move the insertion point to the location where the package is to be inserted.

6. Pull down the client application's Edit (Alt-E) menu and select Paste (P), or press Ctrl-V. The package is displayed as an icon in the document.

Creating a Package with File Manager

You can use the File Manager or the mouse to create a package and insert it in a document created by a client application. For most applications that support OLE, you need not use Object Packager to embed the document as a package.

Start with both the File Manager and the client application document open and visible on-screen.

1. Click on the directory containing the file you wish to insert, or use the direction keys to highlight the directory and press ⏎. The contents of the directory are displayed in the Content pane.

2. Click on the file in the Content pane, or press Tab and use the direction keys to highlight the file name.

3. With the mouse, drag the file icon from the Content pane of the File Manager to the client application document to package an embedded document. To package a linked document, press Ctrl-Shift while dragging the file icon. The package appears as an icon at the location of the insertion point in the client application document. If you do not have a mouse, pull down the File (Alt-F) menu and select Copy (C), or press F8, and continue with the remaining steps.

4. Select the Copy to Clipboard (Alt-C) option button.

5. Select OK or press ⏎. The file is copied to the Clipboard.

6. Move the insertion point to the location in the client application document where you wish to insert the package.

7. Pull down the Edit (Alt-E) menu and select Paste (P) to embed, or Paste Link (L) to link the package in the

document. The package is displayed as an icon in the client application document.

Working with Part of a Document

To create an object that is part of a document—for example, a portion of a Paintbrush picture—the source document must be produced by a server application. The target document for the package must be produced by a client application.

Once the portion of the source document you wish to package has been copied to the Object Packager, it will be represented by an icon. You can then paste the icon into the target document. If the package is to be linked with another document, the source document file must be saved.

With the server application document and the Object Packager open:

1. Select the portion of the server application document you wish to package.

2. From the application's Edit (Alt-E) menu, select Copy (C), or press Ctrl-C.

3. If it is not already selected, highlight the Content pane of the Object Packager by clicking on it or by pressing Tab.

4. Pull down the Object Packager's Edit (Alt-E) menu and select Paste (P) to embed or Paste Link (L) to link the object. The source application's icon appears in the Appearance pane, and the name of the file appears in the Content pane.

5. Pull down the Edit menu again and select Copy Package (K).

6. Open the target client application document and move the insertion point to where you wish the package to be placed.

7. Select Edit (Alt-E) on the target application document's menu bar and select Paste (P), or press Ctrl-V. The package is displayed as an icon in the target document.

Notes   Any file can be imported into the Object Packager. The package created can be copied only to a document created with a client application.

In some applications, a package may automatically be inserted in the upper-left corner of the window, no matter where you have moved the insertion point.

To view or edit the package contents, double-click the object's icon. Or, select Package Object (O) from the application's Edit menu. In the resulting cascade menu, select Activate Contents (A).

SAVING THE OBJECT

When an object has previously been saved, as happens when an object is imported into the Object Packager, you can save it to a new file. This may be useful if you have changed the package's icon.

With Object Packager open and the panes empty:

1.   Pull down the File (Alt-F) menu and select Import (I). The Import dialog box appears.

2.   Double-click on the file you wish to import. Or, press Tab to move the cursor to the File Names list box, use the direction keys to highlight the file name, and press ↵.

3.   If you wish, change the imported package's icon.

4.   Pull down the File (Alt-F) menu and select Save Contents (S). The Save Contents dialog box appears.

5.   Type a new name for the package in the File Name (Alt-N) text box.

6.   Click OK or press ↵ to save the package to a new file.

UPDATING A PACKAGE

When Object Packager is opened from another application, you can update the package in the document.

1.   Click on the package's icon, or use the direction keys to select the package. Pull down the application's Edit (Alt-E)

menu, select Package Object (O), and select Activate Contents (A). The Object Packager window appears.

2. Change the package according to your needs.

3. Pull down the File (Alt-F) menu and select Update (U). The package in the document is updated to reflect your changes.

4. Close the Object Packager. A message box appears asking if you wish to update your document. Click Yes or press ↵.

See Also Cardfile Operations, Microsoft Write, Paintbrush Features and Operations, the Appendix.

PAINTBRUSH FEATURES AND OPERATIONS

Paintbrush is a Windows drawing program you can use to create, save, modify, and print graphic images. It generates detailed color or black-and-white images that can be used in any other Windows program that supports bit-mapped graphics, including Write. Among other things, Windows can use graphics generated by Paintbrush as wallpaper images for the Windows desktop (see "Changing the Desktop Wallpaper").

The Paintbrush screen is divided into four areas: the Toolbox, the Linesize Box, the Palette, and the Drawing Area (see Figure II.13):

- The *Toolbox* contains symbols representing drawing actions the cursor can perform. Select the straight line and the cursor becomes, in effect, a tool that will draw straight lines; select the filled circle and the cursor will draw filled circles. Other tools cut and paste, enter text, and erase.

- The *Linesize box* lets you set the thickness of the lines drawn by Paintbrush. This setting affects all lines available in Paintbrush. It also determines the eraser and paintbrush widths, and spray-can tool size.

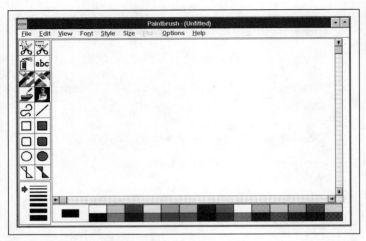

Figure II.13: The Paintbrush screen

- The *Palette* contains a grid showing the various colors you
  can select and use.

- The *Drawing Area* is the workspace where you create your
  Paintbrush drawings.

The Paintbrush icon appears in the Accessories program group. To
start Paintbrush, follow these steps:

1. Open the Accessories program group.

2. Double-click on the Paintbrush icon, or use the direction
    keys to highlight Paintbrush and then press ↵. The
    Paintbrush window will appear.

ADDING TEXT TO A DRAWING

You can add text to the drawing by using the Text tool. The appearance of the text will depend on the foreground color, font, and
font size selected.

1. Click on the Text tool. Or, press Tab until the pointer is in
    the Toolbox, use the direction keys to move the pointer
    to the Text tool, and press Ins.

2. If necessary, pull down the Text (Alt-T) menu and select Fonts (F) to choose a new font and font size in the dialog box, and click OK or press ↵. You can also change the formatting of the text by toggling the text characteristics. (See "Options," below.)

3. Move the cursor to the location where you want to begin the text and click on the mouse button. Or, press Tab to move the cursor to the drawing area, use the direction keys to position the cursor, and press Ins.

4. Type in the text. Use the Backspace key to correct any errors.

Options

Regular (R)—removes all text formatting (the default).

Bold (B)—toggles bold text formatting. Can also be toggled using the Ctrl-B key sequence.

Italic (I)—toggles italic text formatting. Can also be toggled using the Ctrl-I key sequence.

Underline (U)—toggles underlining the text. Use the Ctrl-U key sequence also to toggle underlining.

Outline (O)—if you choose a background color different than that selected for the drawing, the text will appear outlined.

Shadow (S)—if you choose a background color different than that selected for the drawing, a drop-shadow effect will appear on the text.

Fonts (F)—opens the Font dialog box. Select the appropriate options:

> **Font (Alt-F)**—click on the scroll arrows or use the direction keys to highlight the font in the scroll box. As you highlight different fonts, the Font Style and Size options change, and the Sample area reflects the newly selected font's appearance.

> **Font Style (Alt-Y)**—click on the style, or use the direction keys to highlight it in the list box.

> **Size (Alt-S)**—click on the size, or use the direction keys to highlight it in the list box.

> **Strikeout (Alt-K)**

> **Underline (Alt-U)**

THE AIRBRUSH

With the Airbrush tool, you can "spray" the selected foreground color in your drawing. A circular array of dots appears where you have used the Airbrush. The line size selected determines the width of the spray.

1. Click on the Airbrush tool. Or, press Tab until the pointer is in the Toolbox, use the direction keys to move the pointer to the Airbrush tool, and press Ins.

2. Move the cursor to the position you want to begin to spray with the mouse. Or, press Tab until the cursor is in the drawing area and use the direction keys to position the cursor.

3. Click on the mouse button and drag the cursor where you want to spray, then release the mouse button. Or, press and hold Ins, use the direction keys to spray the design, and release the Ins key.

Notes The density of the spray is determined by how quickly you drag the cursor. When you use the direction keys, you can form only horizontal and vertical lines of spray.

BOXES AND CIRCLES

Paintbrush lets you create many different types of shapes—circles, squares, and polygons, to name a few. The eight basic shapes in the Paintbrush Toolbox are the box and the filled box; the rounded box and the filled rounded box; the circle/ellipse and the filled circle/ellipse; and the polygon and the filled polygon. See Figure II.13.

The method for creating all types of boxes and circles is described below. Creating polygons is described in "Polygons."

1. Click on the shape you wish to create. Or, press Tab until the mouse pointer appears in the Toolbox, use the direction keys to select the shape, and press the Ins key.

2. With the mouse, move the pointer out into the drawing
    area to the location where you want the upper-left corner
    of your shape to appear. Or, press Tab until the mouse
    pointer appears as a cross hair at the bottom of the
    Paintbrush workspace, and then press an arrow key to
    position the cursor.

3. Click the mouse button and drag the pointer to the lower
    right corner of your drawing, then release the mouse but-
    ton. Or, press and hold Ins, press the ↓ to move the cross
    hair down, press → to move the cross hair to the rightmost
    edge of the shape, and release the Ins key. The shape will
    appear in the workspace.

Notes   You can control the appearance of shapes a great deal by
setting the line size. See "Line Size."

THE BRUSH TOOL

The Brush tool is the default drawing tool for Paintbrush. It is used
to draw freehand figures. The Brush's size is determined by the line
size selected, and you can also change its shape.

Changing the Shape of the Brush

1. Pull down the Options menu (Alt-O) and select Brush
    Shapes (B), or double-click on the Brush tool. The
    Brush Shapes dialog box appears.

2. Double-click on the shape you wish to use, or use the
    direction keys to select it and press ↵. The Brush tool
    appears in the selected shape.

Drawing with the Brush

With the foreground color, line width, and Brush shape selected:

1. If the Brush is not already selected, click on the Brush tool.
    Or, press Tab until the pointer is in the Toolbox, use the
    direction keys to move the pointer to the Brush, and
    press Ins.

2. Use the mouse to position the cursor in the drawing area. Or, press Tab until the cursor appears in the drawing area, and use the direction keys to position the cursor where you wish to begin your drawing.

3. Click and hold the mouse button, drag the cursor to form your drawing, then release the mouse button. Or, press and hold the Ins key, use the direction keys to draw your shapes, then release the Ins key.

Notes   When you use the direction keys, you can form only horizontal and vertical lines.

CURVES AND LINES

You can add both curved and straight lines to your drawing. Curved lines are created using the Curve tool, and straight lines are formed with the Line tool. With both tools, the selected line width determines the line size, and the lines appear in the selected foreground color.

Drawing Curved Lines

1. Click on the Curve tool. Or, press Tab until the pointer is in the Toolbox, use the direction keys to move the pointer to the Curve tool, and press Ins.

2. Use the mouse to position the cursor in the drawing area. Or, press Tab until the cursor appears in the drawing area and use the direction keys to position the cursor where you wish to begin drawing the line.

3. Click and hold the mouse button, drag the cursor to form a flexible line, and release the mouse button. Or, press and hold the Ins key, use the direction keys to form the flexible line, and release the Ins key.

4. Click the mouse button, drag the cursor in the direction you wish to form the first curve in the flexible line, then release the mouse button. Or, press and hold the Ins key, use the direction keys to drag the cursor, and release the Ins key.

5. If you wish to add another curve, go to step 6. If you do not want another curve in the line, click on the second end of the line, or use the direction keys to move the cursor to the second end of the line and press Ins. Skip step 6.

6. Click and drag the cursor away from the first curve, then release the mouse button. Or, press and hold Ins, use the direction keys to move the cursor away from the first curve, then release the Ins key.

Notes When you release the mouse button or the Ins key after forming the second curve, the line appears in the foreground color. If you wish to redo the curve at any time before you release the mouse button or the Ins key for the second curve, click the right mouse button or press Del to begin again.

Drawing Straight Lines

1. Click on the Line tool. Or, press Tab until the pointer is in the Toolbox, use the direction keys to move the pointer to the Line tool, and press Ins.

2. Use the mouse to position the cursor in the drawing area. Or, press Tab until the cursor appears in the drawing area and use the direction keys to position the cursor where you wish to begin drawing the line.

3. Click and hold the mouse button, drag the cursor to form a flexible line, and release the mouse button. Or, press and hold the Ins key, use the direction keys to form the flexible line, and release the Ins key. The line is pasted in the drawing area.

Notes When you release the mouse button or the Ins key, the line appears in the foreground color. If you wish to redo the line at any time before you release the mouse button or the Ins key, click the right mouse button or press the Del key to begin again. To form a straight line, press and hold the Shift key while you are drawing.

CUTOUTS

A cutout is a portion of a Paintbrush image, defined by the user, that can be deleted, moved, copied, or sized. There are two cutout tools, a rectangular tool called the Pick and a free-form tool called the Scissors.

Once you have selected a cutout, you can use the Cut or Copy option in the Edit menu to place it in Clipboard. You can then paste it into other Windows applications or back into Paintbrush.

You can save the cutout in a file of its own, if you wish, using the Copy To command on the Edit pull-down menu.

Copying a Cutout

You can copy a cutout image to any position you like in the Paintbrush workspace. You can make either a transparent or an opaque copy.

1. Select the cutout by clicking on it, or press Tab to move the cursor into the workspace, use the direction keys to position it over the cutout, and press Ins.

2. To make a transparent copy, press and hold the Ctrl key, and click and drag the cutout to the position where you wish to place the copy. Release the Ctrl key and the mouse button. Or, press and hold the Del-F9 keys, then press an arrow key to copy the cutout to a new location. Release the keys.

3. To make an opaque copy, press and hold the Shift key, then click and drag the cutout with the mouse. Release the Shift key and the mouse button. Or, press Ins-Shift and then an arrow key to make an opaque copy. Release the keys.

4. Click outside the cutout, or use the arrow keys to move the cursor outside the cutout and press Ins to paste the copy of the drawing in the new location.

Creating a Cutout

The rectangular cutout tool, Pick, allows you to define a rectangular section of a Paintbrush image as the cutout; the free-form tool allows you to define a cutout of any shape (though you have to have a steady hand to use it for detailed work).

Using the Rectangular Cutout Tool

1. Click on the Pick. Or, press Tab until the pointer is in the Toolbox, use the direction keys to move the pointer to the Pick, and press Ins.

2. Place the mouse pointer at the upper-left corner of the drawing. Or, press Tab until the cross hair appears in the workspace and use the direction keys to position it at the upper-left corner of the drawing.

3. Click and hold the mouse button, then drag the pointer to the lower-right corner of the area. The outline of a rectangle will appear and move with the pointer. Release the mouse button. Or, press Ins-↓ until the pointer reaches the lower edge of the drawing and, while still pressing Ins, press → to move the cursor to the right edge of the drawing. A rectangular outline will appear. The area within the rectangle is the cutout.

Using the Free-Form Cutout Tool

1. Click on the Scissors tool. Or, press Tab until the pointer is in the Toolbox, use the direction keys to move the pointer to the Scissors tool, and press Ins.

2. Place the mouse pointer at any point on the perimeter of the area you wish to select. Or, press Tab until the cross hair appears in the workspace and use the direction keys to position it on the perimeter.

3. Click and hold the mouse button, then drag the pointer carefully around the area you wish to select. Release the mouse button to define the perimeter. Or, press Ins and an arrow key to define the perimeter. The defined area, surrounded by a dotted line, is the cutout.

Notes   If you release the mouse button or the Ins and arrow keys
before you return to your starting point, Paintbrush will draw a
straight line between the release point and the starting point, pos-
sibly intersecting the image. To redefine your cutout, move the cursor outside of the cutout using the mouse or the direction keys, and
click the mouse button or press Ins.

If you are using the keyboard to define your cutout, your perimeter
will consist of straight lines only.

Deleting a Cutout

To delete a cutout, you must first define it (see "Creating a
Cutout"), then cut it into the Clipboard. If you select Copy instead
of Cut, the original cutout will remain in the Paintbrush workspace
and a copy will be be placed in the Clipboard.

- With the cutout created, pull down the Edit menu (Alt-E)
  and select Cut (T), or press Ctrl-X. The cutout will disappear from the Paintbrush workspace. A copy of it will be
  placed in the Clipboard.

Moving a Cutout

You can move a cutout image to any position you like in the
Paintbrush workspace.

1. Click on the cutout and, while holding the mouse button,
   drag the cutout to the desired location. Release the mouse
   button. Or, press and hold the Ins key and use the arrow
   keys to move the cutout to the desired location. Release
   the keys.

2. Click outside the cutout to paste the drawing in the new
   location. Or, use an arrow key to move the cursor outside
   of the cutout and press Ins to paste the drawing in the
   new location.

ERASING

Paintbrush has two erasing tools—the Eraser, which replaces all
colors with the background color, and the Color Eraser, which

changes a selected color either to the background color or a different color.

The Eraser

The Eraser tool allows you to remove a color. The selected background color fills the erased portion of the drawing. It is easy to confuse the Eraser with the Color Eraser; the Eraser is in the right-hand column of the Toolbox.

1. Select the Eraser tool.

2. Use the mouse or press Tab until the cursor is in the workspace. The cursor will change into a box, the size of which is determined by the line size setting.

3. Using the mouse or the direction keys, position the pointer over the area you wish to erase. Click and hold the mouse button, or press and hold the Ins key. The area directly under the pointer disappears and is replaced by the background color of the drawing.

4. Use the mouse or the direction keys to move the pointer around the part of the image you wish to erase.

5. Release the mouse button or the Ins key.

Erasing Color

Using the Color Eraser, you can change selected areas of one color to another color, or change all occurrences of one color to another color. The color you wish to change is the foreground color, and the desired new color is the background color.

To change a selected color:

1. Select the foreground and background colors. The background color will replace the foreground color.

2. Select the Color Eraser tool.

3. Use the mouse or press Tab repeatedly to move the pointer into the workspace. The pointer will change into a box with a cross hair in it, its size determined by the line size setting.

4. Use the mouse or the direction keys to move the pointer
to the area where you wish to change colors. Click and
hold the mouse button as you move the cursor across the
area, or press and hold Ins while using the direction keys
to replace the foreground color with the background color.
Then release the mouse button or the Ins key.

To change all occurrences of a color:

• Double-click on the Color Eraser tool.

• Or, press the F9-Ins key sequence.

Notes   To move the Color Eraser only horizontally or vertically
with the mouse, hold down the Shift key as you drag the mouse
pointer.

FILL COLORS AND PATTERNS

The Paint Roller is a Paintbrush tool that will fill any enclosed
shape with the selected foreground color or crosshatch pattern. If
used in an unenclosed space, it will fill the entire drawing area with
the new color or pattern.

Start with a shape on the screen to hold the fill color or pattern. See
"Boxes and Circles" or "Polygons."

1. Click on the desired fill color or, if you are working in
black-and-white, the crosshatch pattern. Or, press Tab
until the pointer is in the Palette, use the direction keys to
move the pointer to the color or crosshatch pattern, and
press Ins.

2. Click on the Paint Roller tool. Or, press Tab to move
the pointer to the Toolbox, use the direction keys to
move the pointer to the Paint Roller tool, and press Ins
to select the tool.

3. Use the mouse to move the pointer into the workspace, or
press Tab until the pointer is in the workspace. The
pointer will change into a picture of a paint roller.

4. With the mouse or the direction keys, position the pointed
    tip of the paint roller in the area you wish to fill. Click the
    mouse button, or press the Ins key. The area will fill with
    the specified color or pattern.

Notes   If you selected a crosshatch pattern or a nonsolid color,
you must use the Color Eraser to refill the enclosed shape.

FOREGROUND AND BACKGROUND COLORS

To select different colors for your drawing, you must first define
your foreground and background colors. The default foreground
color is black, and the default background color is white.

To change the foreground color:

- Click on the color you wish to select as the foreground color.
- Or, press Tab until the pointer is in the Palette, use the arrow
  keys to move the pointer to the desired color, and press Ins.

To change the background color:

- Click with the right mouse button on the color you wish to
  select as the background color.
- Or, press Tab until the pointer is in the Palette, use the arrow
  keys to move the point to the desired color, and press Del.

The selected colors appear in the color selection box to the left of the
Palette.

LINE SIZE

Paintbrush will draw lines in varying degrees of thickness. The line
size setting determines the Eraser and Paintbrush widths, and the
Spray Can size—the thinner the line size, the narrower the eraser
and Brush, and the smaller the spray area. You specify line thickness using the Linesize Box.

1. Move the mouse pointer over the Linesize Box, or press
    Tab until the Linesize box is selected. The pointer will
    become an arrow positioned on the right side of the
    Linesize Box.

2. Click on the desired line size, or use the ↑ and ↓ keys to move the arrow up or down until it is beside the line size you want, and then press the Ins key.

POLYGONS

Creating a polygon is slightly different from creating other shapes. You create the sides of the polygon in sequence.

1. Click on the Polygon tool. Or, press Tab to move the pointer to the Toolbox, use the direction keys to move the pointer to the Polygon tool, and press Ins.

2. Use the mouse or press Tab until the cursor is in the drawing area (the pointer will change into a cross hair), and place it at the location where you want to begin the first side of the polygon.

3. Click and hold the mouse button, and drag the pointer to the location where you want the side to end. Release the mouse button. Or, press Ins and an arrow key to move to the end of the first line. Release the Ins key.

4. Starting at the end of the line last defined, repeat step 3 until you have defined all but the last side of the polygon.

5. Double-click the mouse button or press the F9-Ins key sequence. A line will appear between the end of the last line drawn and the starting point of the first line, completing the polygon.

PRINTING FROM PAINTBRUSH

Paintbrush gives you the ability to print an image in draft (low-resolution) or proof (high-resolution) mode. It also lets you print all or part of an image, and generate single or multiple copies.

1. Pull down the File menu (Alt-F) and select Print (P). The Print dialog box will appear.

2. Set the various print options to suit your needs. (See "Options," below.)

3. Click on OK or press ↵. If you chose to print the whole image, you can stop here—Paintbrush will print the image. If you chose in step 2 to print only a part of the image, the Paintbrush workspace will be redrawn to display the entire image and the pointer will become a cross hair. Follow steps 4–5.

4. Using the mouse or the direction keys, move the pointer to the upper-left corner of the area you wish to print.

5. Click and hold the mouse button, and drag the pointer to the lower-right corner of the area. Or, press and hold the Ins key, press ↓ to move the pointer to the lower edge of the area, then press → to move the flexible box to the right edge of the area. Release the mouse button or the Ins key, and Paintbrush will print the selected image.

Options In the Quality area, select from:

Draft (Alt-D)—prints the drawing at the fastest printer speed.

Proof (Alt-P)—prints the drawing at a slower speed, using advanced printer features.

In the Window area, select from:

Whole (Alt-W)—prints the complete drawing.

Partial (Alt-R)—selects a portion of the drawing.

Other options include:

Number of Copies (Alt-N)—type a number in the text box to print more than one copy.

Scaling (Alt-S)—type in a percentage value to print the selected drawing to a scale. 100% is the default.

Use Printer Resolution (Alt-U)—prints the selected drawing at the printer resolution rather than the screen resolution. The printed image may be stretched to produce the screen dimensions.

SAVING A PAINTBRUSH DOCUMENT

Paintbrush will save to a disk file any document you edit. By default, all Paintbrush documents have a .BMP extension, which denotes a Windows bit-map file.

If the file being saved already has a name (because you previously saved it), Paintbrush will not prompt you for the file name. It will store the file to the current file name.

For instructions, see "Saving Files" under "Standard Operations."

SAVING A PAINTBRUSH IMAGE IN A DIFFERENT FORMAT

Windows Paintbrush saves files in five file formats:

- PCX Files—saves Paintbrush files in PCX format.

- Monochrome Bitmap—uses only black and white. When you save a color image to a monochrome bitmap format, all the colors in the image are translated to some type of crosshatching or gray tone.

- 16-Color Bitmap—uses only 16 true colors. Represents all other colors with some mixture of these primary 16.

- 256-Color Bitmap—uses 256 true colors, and can render images with photo-realistic quality. Typically, 256-color bitmap files are about twice the size of 16-color bitmap files.

- 24-Bit Bitmap—allows for a high-resolution display.

You can convert a file to a different format by first opening the file in its source format, and then saving it to a different format. This is a good method for converting color drawings to monochrome: you may want to do this to see how the drawings will appear when printed on a laser printer, and edit them if necessary.

You can also import any graphic image into Paintbrush via the Clipboard and save it as a PCX file. Because the PCX file format is accepted by many different graphics programs, you can use such Paintbrush files in a wide variety of programs.

See "Saving Files under a New Name" under "Standard Operations."

ZOOMING OUT AND IN

The first time you start Paintbrush, it determines a default size for the drawing area. The default size depends on the amount of memory available and the display adapter. Using Zoom Out, you can view an entire picture or paste a graphic that is larger than the default screen size. Paintbrush also lets you edit images very precisely, using Zoom In. Zoom In will magnify a portion of the Paintbrush screen and let you edit individual pixels.

To Zoom Out

When a Paintbrush image is zoomed out, only the Edit, View, and Help menus are available.

1. Pull down the View (Alt-V) menu and select Zoom Out (O), or press Ctrl-O. The Paintbrush workspace will be redrawn to display the entire image area.

2. To cancel Zoom Out, pull down the View (Alt-V) menu and select Zoom In (I), or press Ctrl-N.
   the rectangle, press and hold the Ins key, and move the rectangle using the direction keys.

To Zoom In

1. Pull down the View (Alt-V) menu and select Zoom In (I), or press Ctrl-N. The pointer will change into a rectangle that will mark the area to be magnified.

2. Using the mouse or the direction keys, move the rectangle to cover the area you want magnified, then click the left mouse button or press the Ins key. Click the left mouse button or press Ins to change a pixel to the current foreground color; click the right mouse button or press Del to change a pixel to the current background color. To change an entire group of pixels, click and hold the appropriate button, then drag the pointer over the pixels you wish to change. Or, press and hold the Ins key and use the direction keys. Release the mouse button or Ins key.

3. To cancel Zoom In, pull down the View (Alt-V) menu and select Zoom Out (O), or press Ctrl-O.

PIF EDITOR OPERATIONS

A PIF (*program information file*) contains information that Windows uses to run a standard DOS application in a way that is appropriate for that application. (Even though it is redundant, this is customarily called a PIF file.) A PIF file tells Windows what the program's name is, what kind of video it uses, how much memory it requires, what ports it accesses, and more. Though each non-Windows application should have its own PIF file, Windows comes with a PIF file that contains default PIF settings for the mode you are using. It is called _DEFAULT.PIF and it is located in the Windows directory. These default settings are used if the application doesn't have its own PIF file. You may want to open this file and edit it to suit your needs (see "Opening a PIF File" and "Creating and Editing a PIF File"). Many standard DOS applications, however, are now shipped with a PIF file (you may need to modify it).

The PIF Editor icon appears in the Main program group. To start the PIF Editor, follow these steps:

1. Open the Main program group.

2. Double-click on the PIF Editor icon. The PIF Editor window will appear.

CREATING AND EDITING A PIF FILE

To create a new PIF file or edit an existing one, follow these steps:

1. Run the PIF Editor.

2. Pull down the Mode (Alt-M) menu and select Standard (S) or 386 Enhanced (3) to choose a mode in which to run the application. A message box will appear if you are not currently running Windows in that mode. Click OK or press ↵ to create the PIF file in a different mode.

3. Specify new parameters or edit the existing ones as necessary. (See "Options," below.)

Options   The PIF Editor window contains a series of parameters that you can adjust. These parameters differ, depending on whether you are in Real/Standard modes or 386 Enhanced mode (for an explanation of these modes, see "The Windows Interface" in Part I).

Program Filename—the complete path and name of the program file.

Window Title—the program name you want to appear in the window's title bar.

Optional Parameters—any alphanumeric character string that follows the Program Filename. An optional parameter might be the name of a document or database with which you want the program to work.

Start-up Directory—the directory that the DOS application will address when it starts.

Video Mode—an option available in Real and Standard modes only (Real mode is not available in Windows 3.1). It tells Windows what type of video the application uses so it can allocate the correct amount of video memory. The options available are Text and Graphics/Multiple Text. Text mode uses less memory, and allows the application to use more.

Video Memory—tells Windows how much memory to allocate for use by the video adapter. The available options are Text, Low Graphics, and High Graphics. The Text option requires the least amount of memory of the three; the High Graphics option demands the most. Sometimes a DOS application will change video modes, freeing memory for Windows. When the DOS application then switches back to the original mode, no memory is available for the application. To specify and retain the m aximum amount of video memory, select the High Graphics option button and the Retain Video Memory check box, which is under Display Options in the Advanced 386 Options dialog box.

Memory Requirements—specifies the amount of memory required for the application to run. In 386 Enhanced mode, you can also specify the amount of memory the application would like to have.

XMS Memory—tells Windows how much extended memory to supply to an application that uses the Lotus-Intel-Microsoft-AST extended memory specification. The KB Required option lets you set the minimum extended memory requirement for an application. The KB Limit option lets you specify the maximum amount of extended memory the application is allowed to use.

Display Usage—a parameter available only in 386 Enhanced mode. It tells Windows to run the application using the full screen, or in a window.

EMS Memory—tells Windows how much memory to supply to an application that uses the Lotus-Intel-Microsoft Expanded memory specification. Available only in 386 Enhanced mode. The KB Required option lets you set the minimum expanded memory requirement for an application. The KB Limit option lets you specify the maximum amount of expanded memory the application is allowed to use.

Directly Modifies—tells Windows that the application will attempt to communicate directly with the computer's serial ports and/or the keyboard. This parameter is available only in Real and Standard modes (Real mode is not available in version 3.1).

No Screen Exchange—allows you to "turn off" Windows' ability to cut and paste between DOS applications and Windows, thus freeing up memory for applications. Available only in Real and Standard modes (Real mode is not available in Windows 3.1).

Prevent Program Switch— prevents you from switching back to Windows while the application is executing. This conserves memory. To switch back to Windows, you have to quit the application. Available only in Real and Standard modes (Real mode is not available in Windows 3.1).

Close Window on Exit—tells Windows whether to close a program's window once the program stops running.

No Save Screen—tells Windows not to save video memory for the DOS application when switching between applications. Select this option only if the DOS application can retain its own video memory. Available in Standard mode only.

Reserve Shortcut Keys—allows you to "turn off" certain Windows shortcut keys so that applications can use them (some applications use the same key combinations internally that Windows uses for shortcut keys). This option is available in 386 Enhanced mode, but you have to click on the Advanced command button to get to it.

Execution—available only in 386 Enhanced mode. This parameter allows you to specify whether any applications should run in the background while the current application is in the foreground. The Background option tells Windows to run the current application even when it's minimized. The Exclusive option tells Windows not to run any other applications when this application is running (even if the Execution option for those applications is set to Background).

Multitasking Options—available only in 386 Enhanced mode. Allows you to adjust the multitasking characteristics of an application.

Memory Options—available only in 386 Enhanced mode. Allows you to specify what areas of memory should be used, and to reserve that memory for the application's use.

Display Options—available only in 386 Enhanced mode. Specifies the type of video the application uses so Windows can allocate the correct amount of memory. It also specifies whether Windows should monitor video input and output ports, and whether it should retain video memory once the DOS application switches from a high-resolution display mode to a lower one.

Other Options—lets you change an assortment of settings. Lets you specify whether data can be pasted into an application quickly; lets you disable certain Windows shortcut key sequences, such as Alt-Esc, in case they are used by the application; lets you specify a new shortcut key sequence that will switch to the application; and lets you allow Windows to close the program—terminate it—even if it is still active.

OPENING A PIF FILE

If the PIF file you are opening was generated by a Windows version earlier than 3.0, you will see a warning dialog box; the versions are incompatible. Windows will convert the old format to the new format.

You will need to open a PIF file only to check or edit the settings. See "Opening a File" under "Standard Operations."

SAVING A PIF FILE

After you have created or edited a PIF file, you will need to save it. PIF files are saved with the .PIF extension. See "Saving Files" under "Standard Operations."

PRINT MANAGER OPERATIONS

The Print Manager is a Windows program that automatically manages all printing done by Windows applications.

When you direct a Windows application to print information, the application formats the information for the default printer and stores it in a *print file*, which is then passed to the Print Manager. The Print Manager accepts print files from Windows applications and sends them to the printer. It can accept multiple print files, prioritize them, and send them to the printer one after the other. A series of print files waiting to be printed is called the *print queue*. Using the Print Manager you can change the order of the queue, delete print files from the queue, or pause and resume printing.

The Print Manager window is somewhat similar to the Help window: it, too, has command buttons located below the menu bar. See Figure II.14.

When a file from the queue is being printed, it is listed at the top of the Print Manager workspace with a small picture of a printer next to it. The next file in the list has a 2 next to it, indicating it is the second file in the queue. The next file has a 3, and so on. Information on the size of the print file and the time it was submitted to the Print Manager appears along with the file name.

The Print Manager runs automatically whenever you print a file in Windows. It shuts down when there are no more files to print. You

Figure II.14: The Print Manager screen

will rarely need to run the Print Manager by clicking on its icon, as you would most other Windows programs. Windows does allow you to run the Print Manager in this manner, however, because the Print Manager itself may need adjustments.

1. Open the Main program group.

2. Double-click on the Print Manager icon, or use the direction keys to highlight Print Manager and press ↵. The Print Manager window will appear.

CHANGING THE PRINTING SPEED

When the Print Manager and a Windows application operate simultaneously, some of the computer's processing power is allocated to each program. The Windows application gets more processing power—has a higher priority—than the Print Manager because the Print Manager operates in the background, sending bits of information to the printer when Windows applications are momentarily idle. If you wish to change this, you can configure the Print Manager so that it has priority equivalent to or higher than that of any executing Windows applications. This speed up printing, but will slow down the applications.

1. Run the Print Manager, or maximize the Print Manager if it is already running in a minimized state.

2. Pull down the Options menu (Alt-O).

3. Let the default, Medium Priority (M), remain selected if you want the Print Manager and Windows applications to have equal access to Windows' processing power. Select High Priority (H) if you want the Print Manager to have the most processing power. Select Low Priority (L) if you want it to have the least.

4. Close the Print Manager, or minimize it if a file is still printing.

CHANGING PRINT MESSAGES

The Print Manager is designed to operate in the background, allowing you to continue working while your document prints. The Print Manager will send you messages if, for some reason, you are required to take action. Using the Options menu, you can control what kind of messages the Print Manager displays and when it displays them. To change how the Print Manager displays messages, do the following:

1. Run the Print Manager, or maximize the Print Manager if it is currently running in a minimized state.

2. Pull down the Options menu (Alt-O).

3. Select Alert Always (A), Flash if Inactive (F), or Ignore if Inactive (I). (See "Options," below.)

4. Close the Print Manager or minimize it if a file is still printing.

Options   There are three ways in which the Print Manager can display messages:

Alert Always—the Print Manager will interrupt your work session and display a message box requesting user interaction.

Flash if Inactive—if the Print Manager is minimized or open but inactive, it will cause the computer to beep and then make the Print Manager icon flash, indicating that user interaction is needed (the default).

Ignore if Inactive—the Print Manager will ignore the condition that requires user interaction unless the Print Manager window is active. Printing will stop.

PRINT QUEUES

When multiple files are passed to the Print Manager, they are placed in the print queue and printed in the order received.

Changing the Order of the Print Queue

Using the Print Manager, you can change the order of files not currently printing in a local print queue, and thus change the order in which they will be printed. You cannot change the order of the first file in the queue.

1. Maximize or activate the Print Manager window.

2. Click on the name of the file and hold the mouse button, drag the cursor to the new queue position, and release the mouse button. Or, use the direction keys to highlight the file you wish to move, press and hold the Ctrl key, move the cursor to the new queue position, and release the Ctrl key.

Deleting a File from the Print Queue

After you have submitted a print file to the Print Manager, you may change your mind and decide not to print it. To stop the file from printing, you must delete it from the print queue.

1. Maximize or activate the Print Manager window.

2. Click on the file you wish to delete from the print queue, or use the direction keys to select it.

3. Click on the Delete command button or press Alt-D. A dialog box will appear, asking you to confirm the deletion.

4. Click on OK or press ↵.

Notes   If you delete a file from the queue while it is being printed, you may leave information in the printer buffer. To remove this data from the buffer, turn the printer off and then on again after deleting the file from the queue. If you are using a printer with a tractor feed, don't forget to align the top of the new page with the print head.

Pausing and Resuming Printing

There may be times when you want to pause the processing of the print queue so you can examine the files in the queue, move them, or delete them. The Print Manager allows you to do this with the Pause command. When the current file finishes printing, the next file in the queue will not automatically start printing. The Print Manager's Pause command does *not* allow you to stop the current print file from printing, unless you are printing on a network that permits such interruptions.

1.   Maximize or activate the Print Manager window.

2.   Select the current printer by clicking on its name, or use the direction keys to highlight it.

3.   Click on the Pause command button or press Alt-P. Queue processing will stop.

4.   Click on the Resume command button or press Alt-R to resume queue processing.

Network Print Queues

Viewing an Entire Network Queue

When you use Windows to print to a network printer, the Print Manager workspace by default displays only the files *you* have sent to the printer. However, you can also view the entire network printer queue by following these steps:

1.   Run the Print Manager, or maximize the Print Manager if it is currently running in a minimized state.

2.   To select the network printer, click on the information line that describes that printer or use the direction keys to highlight it.

3. Pull down the View menu (Alt-V).

4. Click on Selected Net Queue or press Alt-S. A dialog box displaying the contents of the network will appear.

5. Click on Close or press ↵ when you are done.

Viewing Other Network Queues

If you are using Windows on a network, you have the option of viewing not only the network queue to which you are connected, but other queues as well.

1. Run the Print Manager, or maximize the Print Manager if it is currently running in a minimized state.

2. Pull down the View (Alt-V) menu and select Other Net Queue (O). The Other Net Queue dialog box will appear, asking you to type the network path name of the print queue you wish to view.

3. Type the network path name in the Network Queue (Alt-N) text box.

4. Click on View (Alt-V) or press ↵. The Print Manager will display network queue information in a box above the Network Queue dialog box.

Updating Network Queues

Network queue information that appears in the Print Manager is updated at regular intervals, which are determined by your network software. You have the option of manually updating the network queue information to see the current state of the queue.

1. Run the Print Manager, or maximize the Print Manager if it is currently running in a minimized state.

2. Pull down the View menu (Alt-V) and select Refresh (R), or press F5. The network queue information will be updated.

DISPLAYING THE
TIME/DATE SENT AND THE FILE SIZE

When a file is sent to the Print Manager, the file's name and the name of the program that originated it are displayed. By default, the time and date the file was sent to the Print Manager and the size of the print file are also displayed. You can toggle off the display of the time and date sent and the print file size.

1. Maximize or activate the Print Manager window.

2. Pull down the View (Alt-V) menu and select Time/Date Sent (T) or Print File Size (P).

Notes Once you select either option, the View menu will close. You must pull it down again to select the other option. When toggled on, a check mark appears in front of the option.

PROGRAM GROUPS AND GROUP WINDOWS

Within the Program Manager window, there are secondary windows called *group windows*. They appear on the screen either as open windows containing icons or as group icons (see Figure II.15). Group icons cannot be moved outside the Program Manager window, and they always appear as shaded rectangles with tiny icons inside.

Group windows organize programs into discrete, related sets. One group window, for example, may contain all programs associated with word processing, while another may be for telecommunications. Windows comes with five default group windows: Main, Accessories, Games, Applications, and StartUp.

When a group window is open, the icons for the programs you can run are displayed within. You can maximize or minimize group windows, add programs to them, delete programs from them, and move or copy programs between them.

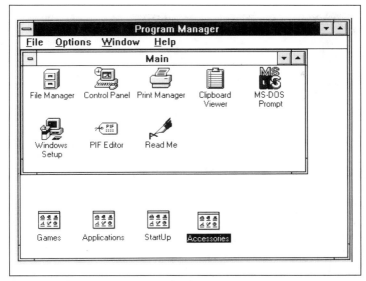

Figure II.15: The Program Manager window

ADDING A GROUP WINDOW

There are many reasons to add (create) a new group window. You may have installed a new type of software on your hard disk and now need a group window to keep it organized. Or you may want to organize your old programs in a new way—for example, by placing all your word processing programs in single group window.

1. Pull down the Program Manager File menu (Alt-F) and select New (N). The New Program Object dialog box will appear.

2. If it is not selected already, click on the Program Group (Alt-G) option button. Then click OK or press ↵. The Program Group Properties dialog box will appear.

3. Type the name you wish to appear below the group icon and in the group window title bar in the Description (Alt-D) text box.

4. If you wish, type the path and file name for the new group in the Group File (Alt-G) text box.

5. Click OK or press ↵ to create the new group window.

Notes   The Program Manager will automatically generate a file name with a .GRP extension if you do not enter a path in the Group File text box. If you wish to select your own file name, follow the DOS file name format.

ADDING A PROGRAM TO A GROUP

There are many reasons to add a program to a group window. You may have purchased new software that you wish to make accessible from Windows, or you may have old software that you wish to invoke from Windows.

There are two ways to add a program to a group window. You can use the File Manager to display a list of files, and then drag the desired program file into the group window; or you can use the Program Manager's menu system to key in the name of the program you want to add to the group. The first method is explained under "File and Directory Management." The second is described below.

1.   Open the group window to which you wish to add a program.

2.   Pull down the Program Manager's File menu (Alt-F) and select New (N). The New Program Object dialog box will appear.

3.   Click on the Program Item (Alt-P) option button if it is not already selected. Then click OK or press ↵. The Program Item Properties dialog box appears.

4.   Type the name you wish to appear below the program's icon and in the program's title bar.

5.   Press Tab or Alt-C to move the cursor to the Command Line text box. Type in the program's path, including the file name and extension. Use the Browse (Alt-B) button to search for the path.

6.   If you wish, press Tab or Alt-W to move the cursor to the Working Directory text box. Type in the drive and directory name that the program will use to store its program files.

7. If you wish, press Tab or Alt-S to move the cursor to the Shortcut Key text box. Press any combination of the Ctrl, Alt, and Shift keys with a character key to enter the shortcut key combination into the text box.

8. If you want the application to run as an icon on the Windows desktop, enable the Run Minimized (Alt-R) option.

9. Click OK or press ⏎ to add the program to the group window.

Notes If you do not enter a working directory, the Program Manager will automatically generate the path for you.

There is an additional command button in the Program Item Properties dialog box, called Change Icon. See "Changing a Program Icon."

CHANGING A PROGRAM ICON

Every program available under Windows is represented by an icon on the screen. Each icon for a Windows program is stored in that program's file—WRITE.EXE, for example, contains the distinctive Windows Write icon. Some program files house multiple icons. To display the alternate icon for a given program, or to display an icon from a different program file, simply reconfigure the Windows Program Manager.

The default icon for any DOS application is a terminal screen (or sometimes a simple rectangle) with a blue background and the words *MS DOS*. You can also use the Program Manager to assign an icon to any DOS application. Files that contain nothing but icons are available both commercially and through public bulletin boards and online system.

The following instructions apply to DOS and Windows programs alike.

1. Select the program whose icon you wish to change.

2. Pull down the Program Manager's File menu (Alt-F) and select Properties (P), or press Alt-⏎. The Program Item Properties dialog box appears.

3. Click on Change Icon (Alt-I). The Change Icon dialog box appears, listing the name of the file from which the current icon is drawn. The lower half of the dialog box contains a scroll box displaying all the icons in the file.

4. If the icon you wish to change to is in a different file, click on the Browse (Alt-B) button to conduct a search for it. If the icon is in the current file, click on the scroll bar to find it and then double-click on the icon to select it, or use the direction keys to highlight the icon and press ↵.

5. Click OK or press ↵ to close the Program Item Properties dialog box and accept the new program icon.

Notes If the program file whose icon you wish to change does not contain an icon, the Change Icon message box appears. Click OK or press ↵ to select an icon from the PROGMAN.EXE file in step 3. You can then follow the remaining steps to select a new icon.

COPYING AND MOVING PROGRAMS BETWEEN GROUPS

The Windows Program Manager allows you to create your own program groups and place programs in those groups. To help with this, you have the option of copying programs between groups.

To use the mouse:

1. Open the group window containing the program you wish to copy.

2. Open the group window that you wish to contain the copy.

3. If you wish to copy the program, press and hold the Ctrl key.

4. If you wish to copy the program, "grab" the icon of the program you wish to copy by clicking the mouse button and holding it down.

5. Drag the icon to the destination group window, then release the mouse button and the Ctrl key.

To use the keyboard:

1. Open the group window containing the program you wish to copy and highlight the program name.

2. Pull down the Program Manager's File (Alt-F) menu and select Copy (C) or Move (M). The Copy Program Item or Move Program Item dialog box appears.

3. Press the To Group (Alt-T) arrow button or press Alt-↓ to reveal the drop-down list. Use the direction keys to highlight the name of the group window where you wish to place a copy of or move the program and press Alt-↑.

4. Press ↵ to copy or move the program to the new group window.

DELETING A GROUP WINDOW

When you eliminate all the programs of a particular group from your hard disk, you should delete the group window that housed them. Deleting a group window automatically deletes all the program icons within that group.

1. Close the group window you wish to delete and make it a group icon. (If you attempt to delete an open group window, Windows will assume you want to delete the currently selected program item.)

2. Highlight the group icon of the group window you wish to delete.

3. Pull down the Program Manager's File menu (Alt-F) and select Delete (D), or press the Del key. You will see a message box asking you if you really wish to delete the selected group window.

4. Select Yes or press ↵.

DELETING A PROGRAM ICON FROM A GROUP

When you delete a program file from your hard disk, you should also delete the program item (the icon) from the group window, since it no longer serves any purpose.

1. Open the group window that contains the program icon you wish to delete.

2. Select the program icon by clicking on it once, or use the direction keys to highlight it.

3. Pull down the Program Manager's File menu (Alt-F) and select Delete (D), or press the Del key. You will see a dialog box that asks you to confirm the item icon's deletion.

4. Select Yes or press ↵.

Notes   It is worthwhile to keep in mind that when you delete a program icon, you do not delete the program it invokes.

MAXIMIZING A GROUP WINDOW

To maximize a group window is to make it expand within the Program Manager window so that it takes up the entire window.

*   Place the mouse pointer on the Maximize button in the upper-right corner of the group window and click the left mouse button. Keyboard users should press Alt-Hyphen, and then type **X**. The group window will expand to take up the entire Program Manager window.

MINIMIZING A GROUP WINDOW

To minimize a group window is to reduce it to an icon that appears at the bottom of the Program Manager window.

*   Click on the Minimize button in the upper-right corner of the group window. Keyboard users should press Alt-Hyphen, and then type **N**. The group window will be reduced to an icon, which will appear at the bottom of the Program Manager window.

RESTORING A GROUP WINDOW

When the Program Manager is first opened, only one group window will be open. All the others are displayed in the form of group icons (see Figure II.15). By restoring a group icon, you can change it into an open group window.

- Double-click on the group icon you wish to restore, or press Ctrl-Tab repeatedly until the icon is highlighted, then release the Ctrl-Tab keys and press ⏎.

RESTORING A MAXIMIZED GROUP

When a group window is maximized, the upper-right corner of the Program Manager window displays three buttons: a Minimize button, a Maximize button, and a Restore button. The Minimize and Maximize buttons act upon the Program Manager window as a whole, and do not affect group windows. The Restore button, however, reduces the maximized group window to its original size. If you maximized the current group window when it was a group icon, the Restore button will not turn it back into an icon; it will make it an open window.

- Click on the Restore button in the upper-right corner of the group window. Keyboard users should press Alt-Hyphen, and then type **R**.

THE STARTUP GROUP

The StartUp program group was automatically created when you set up Windows 3.1. Any application in the group will start when Windows is started. You can add, move, or copy applications into the group window from either Program Manager or File Manager. (See "Adding a Program to a Group," "Copying and Moving Programs between Groups," and "Copying or Moving a File or Directory.")

Dr. Watson

Windows 3.1 includes a small program, Dr. Watson, used for checking for errors in your system. If Dr. Watson is not in your StartUp group window (the Dr. Watson icon will appear in the lower-left corner of the desktop if the program is in StartUp), you can add the program to the StartUp group by using File Manager. (See "Copying and Moving a File or Directory.")

Dr. Watson keeps a record of each startup and any errors detected during a Windows 3.1 session. If an error is detected while you are running an application, a message box is displayed. You can select Ignore, and the message will tell you to save your work to a new file name. Or, you can select Close, which will end the application.

SWITCHING BETWEEN GROUPS

When there are multiple groups on-screen, whether they are group windows or group icons, you may want to switch from one group to another. When you switch groups, the currently active group becomes inactive, and the new group—the one you have switched to—becomes active. You can distinguish the currently active group window by its colored title bar and border.

- Click on the group window, or double-click on the group icon you wish to make active. If you are using a keyboard, press Ctrl-Tab repeatedly until the group you wish to make active is highlighted and then press ↵.

RECONFIGURING WINDOWS WITH SETUP

Setup is a program that allows you to reconfigure Windows for a new type of display, keyboard, mouse, or local area network (LAN). You can also use Setup to install standard DOS applications into the Windows environment.

When Setup is run from within the Windows environment, it functions as a Windows program: it has a program icon, uses menus and dialog boxes, and does everything you would expect. When you run Setup from the DOS command line, it comes up in character mode and displays the same screens and prompts that appeared when you installed Windows for the first time. Setup operates in this character-based mode for two reasons. First, if Windows is currently set up for a graphics display that is not present, or if the driver for the display you want to set up is in use, you can use character-mode Setup to reconfigure Windows for the current display. Second, you can install a device driver that was not shipped with Windows, or an updated version of a device driver that has already been installed.

The Setup program icon is located in the Main program group. During the process of reconfiguring Windows, Setup will request that you insert some of the original Windows installation disks in the computer's floppy-disk drive, so keep the disks handy. After you use Setup, you must exit Windows and then restart it for the change to take effect.

1.   Open the Main program group.

2.   Double-click on the Setup icon, or use the direction keys to highlight it and press ↵.

When Setup is first run, the window depicted in Figure II.16 appears, with the information for your system displayed.

You cannot interact with the information displayed. To make changes, you use the Options menu.

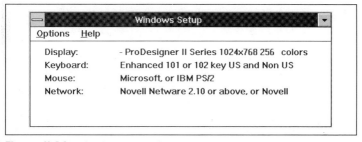

Figure II.16: The Setup window

HARDWARE AND NETWORK RECONFIGURATION

If you change any of the hardware that was present when you installed Windows, or if you add a network, you must reconfigure Windows to recognize the different hardware or network software.

The Windows Setup program will allow you to install any drivers that were included with Windows. If you wish to install drivers that were not included with Windows, you must exit to DOS and run Setup from the DOS prompt.

You can change the display, keyboard, mouse, and/or network drivers that are currently installed.

1. With the new hardware installed, run Windows Setup.

2. Pull down the Options menu (Alt-O) and select Change System Settings (C). The Change System Settings dialog box appears.

3. Click on the arrow button for the setting you wish to change, or use the key sequence to choose Display (Alt-D), Keyboard (Alt-K), Mouse (Alt-M), or Network (Alt-N), and then press Alt-↓ to reveal the setting's drop-down list.

4. Use the scroll buttons or the direction keys to move through the list and highlight the new driver.

5. Click OK or press ↵. The Windows Setup dialog box will appear, asking you to insert one or more (one at a time) of the original Windows disks.

6. Insert each disk specified in the floppy-disk drive and click on OK or press ↵. When the needed files have been installed, the Exit Windows Setup dialog box will appear.

7. Click on Restart Windows (Alt-R) or press ↵ to exit and then restart Windows. Click on Continue (Alt-C) to set up additional system drivers. When Windows restarts, it will expect to find the hardware or network you specified.

Notes   If the hardware or network selected in step 4 was specified when you installed Windows, the driver may already be on the hard disk. If this is the case, you can choose to use the current driver or to install a new driver.

SOFTWARE INSTALLATION

Adding or Removing Windows Files

Windows 3.1 allows you to add files you may not have installed when
you installed Windows. You can also remove files you are not using, in
order to save space on your hard disk. You can add or remove all of the
files or only selected files for a Windows component.

To add all files:

1. Run the Windows Setup program.

2. Pull down the Options (Alt-O) menu and select
    Add/Remove Windows Components (A). The Windows
    Setup dialog box is altered.

3. To add a component previously removed or not installed,
    enable the component by clicking on it or using the key
    sequence (see "Options," below).

4. Click OK or press ↵. The Windows Setup dialog box asks
    you to insert one of the original Windows disks in a disk
    drive. If you need to use a different floppy-disk drive, type
    the drive letter in the text box. Click OK or press ↵.

5. The files are copied to your hard disk. Close the Windows
    Setup program by double-clicking on its control icon, or
    pressing Alt-F4.

To add selected files:

1. Run the Windows Setup program.

2. Pull down the Options (Alt-O) menu and select
    Add/Remove Windows Components (A). The Windows
    Setup dialog box is altered.

3. Click on the Files command button next to the component.
    Or, press Tab until the first Files button is selected, press ↓
    to move the cursor to the Files button next to the com-
    ponent whose files you wish to add, and press ↵. The *Com-
    ponent Name* dialog box appears.

4. To add selected files, click on the file names in the Do Not In-
    stall These Files list box. Or, press Alt-N to move the cursor

to the list box, use the direction keys to move the cursor, and press Spacebar to highlight a file name. You can select more than one file.

5. Click Add or press Alt-A. The files are moved to the Install These Files On The Hard Disk (Alt-I) list box.

6. Click OK or press ⏎ to remove the *Component Name* dialog box.

7. Click OK or press ⏎ to add the selected files. The Windows Setup dialog box asks you to insert one of the original Windows disks in a disk drive. If you need to use a different floppy-disk drive, type the drive letter in the text box. Click OK or press ⏎.

8. The files are copied to your hard disk. Close the Windows Setup program by double-clicking on its control icon, or pressing Alt-F4.

To remove all files:

1. Run the Windows Setup program.

2. Pull down the Options (Alt-O) menu and select Add/Remove Windows Components (A). The Windows Setup dialog box is altered.

3. To remove one of the Windows components, disable it by clicking on its check box or using the key sequence (see "Options," below).

4. Click OK or press ⏎. The Confirm Option Delete dialog box appears.

5. Click Yes (Alt-Y) to remove the files individually, Yes To All (Alt-A) to remove all the files at once, or select No (Alt-N) or press ⏎ to prevent each file from being removed. You can cancel the file removal by clicking the Cancel command button or pressing Esc.

6. The files are removed from your hard disk. Close the Windows Setup program by double-clicking on its control icon, or pressing Alt-F4.

To remove selected files:

1.   Run the Windows Setup program.

2.   Pull down the Options (Alt-O) menu and select
     Add/Remove Windows Components (A). The Windows
     Setup dialog box is altered.

3.   Click on the Files command button beside the component.
     Or, press Tab until the first Files button is selected, press ↓
     to move the cursor to the Files button beside the com-
     ponent whose files you wish to remove, and press ↵. The
     Component Name dialog box appears.

4.   To remove files, click on the file names in the Install
     These Files On The Hard Disk list box. Or, press Alt-I to
     move the cursor to the list box, use the direction keys
     to move the cursor, and press Spacebar to highlight a file
     name. You can select more than one file.

5.   Click Remove or press Alt-R. The files are moved to the
     Do Not Install These Files (Alt-N) list box.

6.   Click OK or press ↵. If you removed only some of the
     component's files, the component's check box appears
     gray. If you removed all of the component's files, the com-
     ponent is disabled.

7.   Click OK or press ↵. The Confirm Option Delete dialog
     box appears.

8.   Click Yes (Alt-Y) to remove the files individually, Yes To
     All (Alt-A) to remove all the selected files at once, or select
     No (Alt-N) or press ↵ to prevent each file from being
     removed. You can cancel the file removal by clicking
     the Cancel command button or pressing Esc.

9.   When you have removed the files, click Cancel or press
     Esc to remove the Confirm Option Delete dialog box.

10. Close the Windows Setup program by double-clicking on
     its control icon, or pressing Alt-F4.

Options

Readme Files (Alt-F)—the explanatory text files included in Windows 3.1.

Accessories (Alt-A)—the programs in the Accessories group and their Help files.

Games (Alt-G)—the games included in Windows 3.1 and their Help files.

Screen Savers (Alt-S)—the files required to run the Screen Savers.

Wallpapers, Misc. (Alt-W)—Wallpaper and Sound files installed with Windows 3.1.

Notes When you remove a component, the number of bytes used for that component is changed to 0. When you add a component, the number of bytes used for the component is displayed. In either case, the number of bytes currently used for all Windows components changes to reflect your action.

Setting Up Applications Automatically

One of Setup's most advanced features is its ability to easily set up non-Windows applications to work in the Windows environment. Setup scans all the hard disks in your computer system, looking for programs it recognizes (Setup recognizes most major PC applications), then creates a list of those applications. It presents that list in a dialog box and gives you the option of adding one, a few, or all the applications to the Windows environment. You may need to create a PIF file for an application if Windows does not. (See "Creating and Editing a PIF File.")

1.   Run the Windows Setup program.

2.   Pull down the Options (Alt-O) menu and select Set Up Applications (S). The Setup Applications dialog box appears.

3.   If it is not already selected, click on the Search for Applications option button or use the ↑ key to select it, then click OK or press ↵. The Setup Applications dialog box is altered.

4.   Click on each hard drive in the list box that you wish to search, or use the direction keys to move the cursor to the drive and then press Spacebar to select it. To scan the

drive(s) and directories in the current path, let the Path listing remain highlighted. To deselect a drive or the Path,
click on the highlighted listing or use the direction keys to
move the cursor to it and press Spacebar.

5.   Click Search Now (Alt-S) or press ↵. As Windows con-
ducts the scan, the Setup Applications dialog box may request you to specify the name of an application. Click on
the name in the list box or use the direction keys to highlight the name. Then click OK or press ↵.

6.   Click on the names of the applications you wish to add to
Windows, or press Alt-F to move the cursor to the Applications Found On Hard Disk(s) list box, use the direction
keys to move the cursor to each name you wish to add,
and press Spacebar. (See "Notes," below.)

7.   Click on the Add command button (Alt-A). If you add one
or more applications and then change your mind, remove
them by clicking on their names in the Set Up For Use
With Windows list box. Or, press Alt-S to move the cursor
to the list box, use the direction keys to move the cursor to
each name, and then press Spacebar to highlight the name.
Then click the Remove (Alt-R) command button.

8.   When all of the application names you wish to add are in
the Set Up For Use With Windows list box, click OK or
press ↵ to let Windows set them up. Windows will add
them to the Applications group in Program Manager. You
can move or copy them to a different group if you wish.
(See "Copying and Moving Programs between Groups.")

9.   When you are finished, close the Windows Setup window
by double-clicking on the control icon or selecting Exit (X)
from the Options (Alt-O) drop-down menu.

Notes   You can select multiple applications in steps 6–7. If you
select an application and then choose not to add it, unselect it by
clicking on its name or pressing the Spacebar again. If you want to
add all the applications listed, just click on the Add All command
button (Alt-D).

Setting Up Applications Manually

Windows Setup provides you with the ability to manually specify the exact location and name of an application and the name of program group in which you wish to place it. It will then add the application to the group in the Program Manager.

1. Run the Windows Setup program.

2. Pull down the Options (Alt-O) menu and select Set Up Applications (S). The Setup Applications dialog box appears.

3. Click on the Ask You to Specify an Application option button or use the ↓ key to select it, then click OK or press ↵. The Setup Applications dialog box is altered.

4. Type the path and file name of the application in the Application Path and Filename text box. If you wish to search for the correct file name or path, click the Browse (Alt-B) button.

5. Click on the Add to Program Group arrow button or press Alt-A and then Alt-↓ to reveal the drop-down list of program groups. Click on the group name (use the scroll buttons if necessary) or use the direction keys to highlight the group and press Alt-↑.

6. Click OK or press ↵ to add the program to the specified group.

7. When you are finished, close the Windows Setup window by double-clicking on the control icon or selecting Exit (X) from the Options (Alt-O) drop-down menu.

STANDARD OPERATIONS

One of the advantages of the Windows environment is that all Windows programs follow certain operating conventions, simplifying both program design and user training. The procedures for saving files, opening files, closing files, closing windows, and undoing mistakes are practically identical for all Windows applications.

BROWSING

Browse buttons are found in many dialog boxes, and are used to select a new drive or directory to search for a file of a specified type.

From any dialog box that contains a Browse button, follow these steps to conduct the search:

1. Click on Browse (Alt-B). The Browse dialog box appears.

2. If necessary, click on the List Files of Type arrow button, or press Alt-T and then Alt-↓ to reveal the drop-down list of the types of files you wish to search for. Double-click on the type of file, or use the direction keys to highlight the file type and press ↵.

3. If necessary, click on the Drives arrow button or press Alt-V then Alt-↓ to reveal the drop-down Drives list. Double-click on the drive letter, or use the direction keys to highlight the drive letter and press ↵.

4. If necessary, double-click on the parent directory in the Directories list box. Or, press Alt-D, use the direction keys to highlight the parent directory, and press ↵. A list of the subdirectories of the parent directory is displayed in the Directories list box.

5. To change to a different subdirectory, double-click on the directory in the Directories list box, or use the direction keys to highlight the directory and press ↵. The list of files of the specified type in the selected directory is displayed in the File Name list box.

6. Double-click on the file name. Or, press Alt-N and then Tab to move the cursor to the File Name list box, use the direction keys to highlight the file name, and press ↵.

CLOSING A FILE

When you close a file, you clear the contents of the current application's window from both the screen and memory.

Only one file at a time can be opened in the applications included in Windows. Windows closes the currently open file when you open another file. Other Window's applications, which are capable of having more than one file open at the same time, use the Close command to close the file displayed in the active window.

1. Open a new file in one of the included Windows applications (see "Opening a File"), or pull down the File menu of an application (Alt-F) not contained in Windows and select Close (C). If you have not saved the current data, a message box will appear asking if you wish to save it.

2. If you do not wish to save the data, select No (Alt-N). The file will close. If you do wish to save the data, go to step 3.

3. Save the data if desired by selecting Yes (Alt-Y) or pressing ↵. If the data has been previously saved, the application will write the data to disk under the old file name. If the data has not been saved, a dialog box will appear asking you for a name.

4. Key in a file name, then click on OK or press ↵ to save the file to the current directory.

CLOSING A WINDOW

To close a window is to render it inactive, at which time the window no longer appears on the desktop. If you close the Program Manager, Windows will stop running and you will be returned to the DOS prompt. If you close a group window, the group is reduced to an icon on the desktop. If the window being closed is an application program, the program ceases running. If a document window is closed in applications that can have more than one file open at a time, the file contained in the window is closed (see "Closing a File").

There are several ways to close a window.

• Double-click on the Control icon of the window you wish to close.

• Press Ctrl-F4 to close a group or document window.

• Press Alt-Hyphen and use the direction keys to highlight Close (C) to close a group or document window.

• Press Alt-F4 to close the Program Manager or an application window.

- Press Alt-Spacebar and use the direction keys to highlight Close (C) to close the Program Manager or an application window.

- If the window is reduced to an icon, click on the icon to reveal the Control menu, and select Close(C). Or, press Alt-Esc until the icon's description is highlighted, then press Alt-Hyphen (for a group or document window) or Alt-Spacebar (for an application window) to reveal the Control menu and select Close (C).

GETTING TO DOS

Sometimes you may find it convenient to be able to go to the DOS prompt without leaving (and then having to restart) Windows. You can run DOS commands or programs using the Run command in Program Manager or File Manager, or you can go to the DOS prompt using the icon in the Main program group.

Do not run any program that may change the file allocation table of your hard disk while you are in Windows. Some of the programs to avoid running while you are in Windows are the CHKDSK/F DOS command, file compaction programs, or disk optimization programs.

To go to the DOS prompt:

1. Open the Main program group.

2. Double-click on the MS-DOS Prompt icon. Or, use the direction keys to highlight MS-DOS Prompt and press ↵. The Windows desktop disappears, and the DOS prompt appears.

To return to Windows:

- From the DOS prompt, type **exit** and then press ↵.

- Press Alt-Tab to switch back to Windows. The MS-DOS Prompt icon appears on the desktop.

- Press Alt-↵ to switch the DOS prompt from full-screen display and to a window, or vice versa.

MOVING WINDOWS AND ICONS

Every window (except windows that are maximized to full screen) or icon that appears on your screen can be moved to a different location. Dialog boxes that have a title bar are also movable windows.

To use the mouse:

•   Click on the icon or the title bar of the window and drag it to the new position on the desktop. Release the mouse button.

To use the keyboard:

1.   Click on the Control icon of the window, or click on the icon to display the Control menu. Or, press Alt-Esc until the window or icon is highlighted, then press Alt-Hyphen (for a document window or icon) or Alt-Spacebar (for a group or application window or icon or a dialog box) to pull down the Control menu.

2.   Select Move (M) on the Control menu. The pointer appears as a four-headed arrow.

3.   Use the direction keys to reposition the window or icon. A rectangle the same size as the window or dialog box moves as you press the direction keys.

4.   When you have placed the window or icon where you wish, press ↵.

Notes   You can undo your move at any time before you release the mouse button or press ↵, by pressing Esc.

OPENING A FILE

To open a file is to read in data from disk and load that data into the current program. Usually, the data read off the disk appears in the application workspace—an image may appear in Paintbrush or a text file in Windows Write. Sometimes opening a file means to open a configuration file that controls how a program operates. Consult your application's documentation to determine what opening a file means for that application.

When you open a file for one of the included Windows applications, the currently open file is closed.

To open a file for one of the applications included with Windows 3.1, follow these steps:

1. Pull down the File (Alt-F) menu of the Windows application and select Open (O). The Open dialog box appears.

2. If necessary, click on the List Files of Type arrow button, or press Alt-T and then Alt-↓ to reveal the drop-down list of the type of file you wish to open. Click on the type of file, or use the direction keys to highlight the file type and press ↵.

3. To select a new drive, click on the Drives arrow button or press Alt-V then Alt-↓ to reveal the drop-down Drives list. Click on the drive letter, or use the direction keys to highlight the drive letter and press ↵.

4. To change to a different directory, double-click on the root directory in the Directories list box. Or, press Alt-D, use the direction keys to highlight the root directory, and press ↵. A list of the directories is displayed in the Directories list box.

5. To change to a different subdirectory, double-click on the directory in the Directories list box, or use the direction keys to highlight the directory and press ↵. The list of files of the specified type in the selected directory is displayed in the File Name list box.

6. Double-click on the file name, or press Alt-N and then Tab to move the cursor to the File Name list box, use the direction keys to highlight the file name, and press ↵. The specified file in the selected directory is opened.

SAVING FILES

1. Pull down the File menu of the application (Alt-F) and select Save (S). If you have saved the file before, the application will save your changes to disk with the same file name. If you have not saved the file before, the Save As

dialog box will appear asking you for a file name (see
"Saving Files under a New Name").

2. Key in the name and click on OK or press ↵.

Saving Files under a New Name

If you have not previously saved a file, or if you wish to modify a file
and save it under a new name, you can use the Save As command.

1. Pull down the File (Alt-F) menu of the Windows 3.1 application and select Save As (A). The Save As dialog box
appears.

2. If necessary, click on the save File as Type arrow button, or
press Alt-T and then Alt-↓ to reveal the drop-down list of
file types you can save. Click on the type of file, or use the
direction keys to highlight the file type and press ↵.

3. To save the file to a new drive, click on the Drives arrow
button or press Alt-V then Alt-↓ to reveal the drop-down
Drives list. Click on the drive letter, or use the direction
keys to highlight the drive letter and press ↵.

4. To save the file to a new directory, double-click on the root
directory in the Directories list box. Or, press Alt-D, use
the direction keys to highlight the root directory, and press
↵. A list of the directories is displayed in the Directories
list box.

5. To save the file to a different subdirectory, double-click on
the subdirectory in the Directories list box, or use the direction keys to highlight the subdirectory and press ↵.

6. Click on the File Name text box and type in the new file
name. The file is saved to the specified file name in the
selected directory.

Notes Depending on the application, saving a file does not neces-
sarily mean saving what you see on the screen (although most of the
time this is the case). In Windows Terminal, for example, you may
see a communications session on the screen; when you save the file,
however, you save only the communications parameters for that session, not the words on the screen. It is important to determine what
saving a file means in your application.

SETTING UP A PAGE

Some of the programs included in Windows, such as Cardfile, Notepad, Calendar, and Paintbrush, allow you to specify headers, footers, and margins using the Page Setup command. Unless you specify different settings, the default settings for each program are used to print the page.

1. Pull down the Windows application's File (Alt-F) menu and select Page Setup (T). The Page Setup dialog box appears.

2. If you wish, type a header in the Header (Alt-H) text box. Then press Tab to move the cursor to or highlight the text in the Footer (Alt-F) text box and type in a footer (see "Options," below.)

3. In the Margins area, press Tab or use the key sequence to highlight the text in the appropriate margin text box. Select Top (Alt-T), Bottom (Alt-B), Left (Alt-L), or Right (Alt-R) to type in the new margin setting.

4. Click OK or press ↵ to use the new settings.

Options

&d—adds the current date.

&p—adds the page number.

&A—adds the name of the file being printed.

&l—left-justifies the text in the header or footer.

&r—right-justifies the text in the header or footer.

&c—centers the text (the default) in the header or footer.

&t—adds the time the file was printed.

Notes If your margins are set too small to print a Paintbrush drawing, a warning message will appear. If the margins are too large, the upper-left corner of the drawing is printed according to the Top and Left margin settings.

SETTING UP THE PRINTER

The document that is currently open in Windows can be printed
either to the printer or to a file.

1. Click on File (Alt-F) to pull down the application's menu,
    and select Print (P). For most Windows applications, the
    Print dialog box will appear.

2. The default printer is listed in the Printer area. If you wish
    to change the default printer, click Setup (Alt-S) to open
    the Print Setup dialog box, and choose a different installed
    printer (see "Changing Printers").

3. In the Print Range area of the Print dialog box, click on the
    option button of the range of the document you wish to
    print (see "Options," below).

4. To change the Print Quality setting, click on the arrow but-
    ton or press Alt-Q and then Alt-↓ to reveal the drop-down
    list. Click on the selection or use the direction keys to high-
    light the selection and then press Alt-↑.

5. If you wish to print the document to a file, click on the
    Print to File check box or press Alt-L.

6. To print more than one copy of the document, click and
    drag the mouse across the Copies text box or press Alt-C
    to highlight the text box and type in a new number.

7. If your printer supports it, you can collate the copies by
    leaving the Collate Copies option enabled. To disable the
    option, click on it or press Alt-I.

8. Click OK or press ↵ to accept the changes and print the
    document.

Options

All (Alt-A)—(the default) prints the entire document.

Selection (Alt-E)—if you have selected text in the document,
you can choose to print only the text selected.

Pages (Alt-P)—allows you to print a continuous range of pages
of the document. Specify which pages to print by typing a
beginning page number in the From (Alt-F) text box and an ending page number in the To (Alt-T) text box.

Notes   If the Windows application has a Page Setup command, not all of the options will be available in the Print dialog box. The Print dialog box in Paintbrush contains options specific to Paintbrush: see "Printing from Paintbrush."

Changing Printers

If you have installed more than one printer, you can select a printer other than the default to print your document. You can also change some of the printer options such as the size of the paper, the page orientation, and the paper source. Each printer driver has its own unique options, so not all options are available for all printers. Windows programs that have a Page Setup command will also have slightly different options.

1. Click File (Alt-F) to pull down the File menu, and then select Print Setup (R). The Print Setup dialog box will appear.

2. In the Printer area of the dialog box, click the option button to select the current Default Printer (the default option) or press Alt-D. The current printer and the port to which it is connected is shown under the Default Printer option.

3. Or, to select a different installed printer, click the Specific Printer option button (Alt-P) and then click the arrow button or press Alt-↓ to reveal the list of installed printers. Click on a printer name, or use the direction keys to highlight the printer name and then press Alt-↑.

4. Make any changes desired to the settings (see "Options," below).

5. Click OK or press ↵.

Options

Paper Size (Alt-Z)—click on the arrow button or press Alt-↓ to reveal the drop-down list of available paper sizes in inches or millimeters. Click on the paper size or use the direction keys to highlight the desired paper size.

Paper Source (Alt-S)—click on the arrow button or press Alt-↓ to reveal the drop-down list of paper sources. Click on the paper source or use the direction keys to highlight the paper source and then press ↑.

Orientation—select Portrait (Alt-R) to make the text or graphic appear upright on a page taller than it is wide. Select Landscape (Alt-L) to make the text or graphic appear upright on a page wider than it is tall.

Options Command Button (Alt-O)—reveals unique options for each printer driver. These may include:

Dithering—select None (Alt-E) to turn dithering off, Coarse (Alt-O) if your resolution is higher than 299 dpi, or Fine (Alt-F) if your resolution is set to less than 200 dpi.

Line Art (Alt-L)—use this option to print defined edges between black, gray, and white if you are not printing in color.

Intensity Control (Alt-I)—use the scroll box or the direction keys to increase or decrease the opaqueness of your graphics.

Color (Alt-C)—(the default) prints graphics in color. Use one of the dithering options to provide colors in addition to the basic colors your printer will produce.

Print Quality (Alt-Q)—select Letter Quality or Draft from the drop-down list.

Print TrueType as Graphics (Alt-G)—prints TrueType fonts as bitmaps and speeds up printing. Not all printers support this option.

UNDOING A MISTAKE

Most Windows programs store your most recent keystrokes and mouse clicks in memory. This gives those programs the ability to undo, or cancel, your most recent actions. If you delete a word by accident, paint something the wrong color, or execute the wrong command, a quick "Undo" command will put you back where you were before you made the mistake.

• Pull down the application's Edit menu (Alt-E), and select Undo (U). A keyboard shortcut for Undo is usually Ctrl-Z.

TASK LIST OPERATIONS

Task List is a utility program that is available at all times while Windows is running. Its purpose is to help you organize and control all the currently executing applications (called tasks). Using Task List, you can switch to any program, stop a malfunctioning program from running (or end a task), arrange the application icons at the bottom of the Windows desktop, or arrange all the open windows on the desktop in a logical and accessible way.

The Task List can be invoked at any time by pressing Ctrl-Esc, or by double-clicking in any blank area of the Windows desktop. (Do not double-click on any window or icon.) Task List is a dialog box.

Windows also provides keystrokes for switching between applications, and an alternative way of shutting down a program if the Task List doesn't work.

ENDING A TASK

Ending a task will stop an application from executing. The application, and anything it is currently working on (if it is a DOS application), will be eliminated from the Windows desktop. If the work the application is doing has not been saved to disk, that work will be lost.

You should choose to end a task only when the task has permanently halted and will not respond to any keyboard or mouse actions. (To find out how to end a task under normal conditions, see "Closing a Window.") Most of the time, the programs that malfunction in this way are DOS applications executing under Windows. Try using Ctrl-C or Ctrl-Break before you use End Task; *invoking End Task should be a last resort.* If you can't close a malfunctioning DOS application using End Task, try terminating it (see "Terminating a DOS Application").

1. Invoke Task List by pressing Ctrl-Esc, or by double-clicking anywhere on the Windows desktop. Task List will appear, with a list box of the currently executing applications within it.

2. Click on the name of the application you want to end, then click on End Task.

See Also   Terminating a DOS Application

SWITCHING TO A TASK

Switching to a task causes the currently active task to become inactive, and the new, selected task to become active.

1. Invoke Task List by pressing Ctrl-Esc, or by double-clicking anywhere on the Windows desktop. Task List will appear, with a list box of the currently executing applications within it.

2. Select the name of the application you want to switch to, then select Switch To (Alt-S). An alternative way of doing this is simply to double-click on the name of the application to which you want to switch.

SWITCHING BETWEEN WINDOWS USING KEY COMMANDS

Windows provides two key commands that allow you to switch quickly between windows: Alt-Esc and Alt-Tab. Unlike Alt-Esc, Alt-Tab also makes the selected window active.

Alt-Esc

Alt-Esc will make the currently active window inactive, and move to the next window in sequence. The sequence is determined by the order in which the programs were last invoked. When you switch to an application icon using Alt-Esc, the icon becomes selected, but nothing else happens. To restore or maximize it, you must double-click on it or invoke its control menu using Alt-Spacebar, then select the option you desire. (To bypass the control menu, see "Alt-Tab.")

1. From anywhere within Windows, press Alt-Esc. The next application in sequence will become selected. If the current application is an icon, the Windows desktop will appear and the icon will be selected.

2. Make the next applications in sequence active by continuing to hold down the Alt key and repeatedly pressing the Esc key.

3. When the application you wish to switch to is selected, release the Alt-Esc keys.

Alt-Tab

In Windows 3.0, Alt-Tab will make the currently active window inactive, move to the next window in sequence, and make it active. The sequence is determined by the order in which the programs were last invoked. In Windows 3.1, a message box appears with the name of the next application in the sequence. Release the Alt-Tab keys to switch to the application whose name is displayed.

When you switch to an application icon using Alt-Tab, the icon becomes selected and is automatically restored to the state it was in before it was minimized. This eliminates the need to invoke the icon's control menu and select Restore.

1. From anywhere within Windows, press Alt-Tab. The next application in sequence is selected.

2. Continuing to hold down the Alt key, repeatedly press the Tab key until the application you desire is selected or its name is displayed.

3. Make the selected application active by releasing the Alt-Tab keys. If the selected application is currently an icon, it will automatically be restored to its original state on the desktop.

TERMINAL COMMUNICATIONS

Terminal is Windows' telecommunications application. It allows you to connect your computer to another computer and exchange information. Using a modem, which connects to the telephone system, Terminal can access information services like CompuServe or MCI Mail.

Terminal has some very advanced communications abilities. You can transmit binary files using the XModem protocol, change the type of terminal that Terminal emulates, or change the screen font. You can also assign keystrokes to the computer's function keys, for example, and then replay those keystrokes by pressing a single key. This allows you to automate log-on procedures or tedious command sequences.

The following instructions assume that you are familiar with basic telecommunications concepts.

1. Open the Accessories program group.

2. Double-click on the Terminal icon, or highlight Terminal by using the direction keys and press ↵. The Terminal window will appear.

BINARY FILES

Downloading a Binary File

To download a binary file is to have another computer send a file to your computer. Before you can receive a file, you must first make sure that both Terminal and the sending computer are using the same transfer protocol. (See "Setting a Binary Transfer Protocol.")

1. Instruct the computer you are communicating with (called the host system) to send a file. The procedure for doing this differs from host system to host system.

2. Pull down the Transfers menu (Alt-T) and select Receive Binary File (F). The Receive Binary File dialog box is displayed.

3. If you wish to send the downloaded file to a different drive, select a different drive letter in the Drives drop-down list box. Click on the arrow button or press Alt-V and then Alt-↓ to reveal the list, then click on the drive letter or use the direction keys to highlight the drive letter and press Alt-↑.

4.   If you wish to place the downloaded file in a different sub-directory, double-click on the directory name, or press Alt-D to move the cursor to the Directories list box, use the direction keys to highlight the directory, and press ↵.

5.   Type a name for the file you wish to download in the File Name (Alt-N) text box. Or, double-click on a file in the list box or press Alt-A then Tab to move the cursor to the list box, use the direction keys to highlight a file name, and press ↵. If you are replacing a file in the selected drive and directory, a message box will appear asking if you wish to overwrite the existing file. Click Yes or press Alt-Y to over-write the file.

6.   Click OK or press ↵ in the Receive Binary File text box. The file transfer will begin. Terminal will display a status line at the bottom of the screen that will indicate how many bytes have been received and how many errors and retries have occurred.

Uploading a Binary File

To upload a binary file is to send a file from your computer to another computer. Before you can send a file, you must first make sure that both Terminal and the receiving computer are using the same transfer protocol. (See "Setting a Binary Transfer Protocol.")

1.   Instruct the computer you are communicating with (called the host system) to receive a file. The procedure for doing this differs from host system to host system.

2.   Pull down the Transfers menu (Alt-T) and select Send Bi-nary File (B). The Send Binary File dialog box will appear.

3.   Type the name of the file you wish to send in the File Name text box, or select the file from the list box. You may want to select a different drive and/or directory from which to select your file (see steps 3–4 above).

4.   Click OK or press ↵ in the Send Binary File dialog box to begin the file transfer. Terminal will display the name of the file and a scale showing the progress of the transfer.

Notes   You can click on the Stop button or press ↲ to stop the download or upload. You cannot select Pause or Resume for a binary file transfer.

Setting a Binary Transfer Protocol

A binary transfer protocol is a set of rules software follows when transferring files between two computers. The software on both the sending and receiving computers must be using the same protocol. Terminal uses two protocols: XMODEM/CRC and Kermit.

1.   Pull down the Settings menu (Alt-S) and select Binary Transfers (B). The Binary Transfers dialog box will appear.

2.   Click on the option button for the desired protocol, or select it using the direction keys.

3.   Click on OK or press ↲.

CHANGING COMMUNICATIONS PARAMETERS

Terminal's communications parameters are the settings that determine how the program communicates with the serial port and modem. All of these settings (see "Options," below) are controlled via option buttons and check boxes in the Communications dialog box.

1.   Pull down the Settings menu (Alt-S) and select Communications (C). The Communications dialog box will appear.

2.   Set the desired communications parameters (see "Options," below).

3.   Click on OK or press ↲.

Options
Baud Rate—a measurement of the speed at which the data is transferred between two modems. Many modems can transfer data at more than one baud rate.

Data Bits—indicates the number of bits in each data packet (character). A bit is a binary digit, either 1 or 0. A character is a group of data bits. A character can be five to eight bits long.

Stop Bits—a specified time interval between the transmitted data packets. The stop bits can be specified as one, one and a half, or two.

Carrier Detect—instructs Terminal to use the modem's carrier detect signal line. If the option is disabled (the default) Terminal uses the modem's response string to see if the modem is connected.

Parity—an error correction scheme used by the serial port. There are five types of parity: even, odd, none, mark, and space. Most systems expect you to use none.

Flow Control—sets the method, or protocol, by which the flow of data is controlled. This setting applies only to terminal emulation and the transmission of textual data; the flow control protocol used for binary file transfers will probably be different. For a software-based protocol, select XON/XOFF. If you select Hardware, the computer's serial port will control the transfer. If you choose None, no protocol will be used.

Connector (serial port)—specifies DOS's name for the serial port you want Terminal to use. DOS serial ports are named COM1, COM2, COM3, and COM4.

Parity Check—specifies whether or not Terminal displays the byte in which a parity error occurred. If this check box is not selected (the default), Terminal simply displays a question mark in place of the byte in which the error occurred. Select this check box only if you are troubleshooting a communications setting and are trying to diagnose a transmission problem.

CHANGING TERMINAL EMULATION

Terminal communicates with larger computer systems by emulating a standard terminal. Terminal emulates three types of terminals: a teletype machine (TTY), the DEC VT-100 (the default emulation), and the DEC VT-52. The VT-100 emulation will also accept standard ANSI control sequences, which are used by most public bulletin boards to draw menus and simple graphics on terminal screens.

1. Pull down the Settings menu (Alt-S) and select Terminal Emulation (T). The Terminal Emulation dialog box will appear.

2. Click on the option button for the desired terminal emulation, or select using the direction keys, then click on OK or press ↵.

CHANGING TERMINAL SETTINGS

The terminal emulation that Terminal uses can be configured in many ways. For example, you can use 80 or 132 columns, and you can specify the font to be used in the emulation. All of these settings (see "Options," below) are accessed using the Terminal Preferences dialog box.

1. Pull down the Settings menu (Alt-S) and select Terminal Preferences (P). The Terminal Preferences dialog box will appear.

2. Change the desired terminal setting (see "Options," below).

3. Click on OK or press ↵.

Options

Line Wrap—specifies whether Terminal will automatically display incoming text on the next line, when that text exceeds the specified column setting. The default setting for Line Wrap is on.

Local Echo—tells Terminal to echo (display) on the screen any character typed at the keyboard. The default setting is for no local echo.

Sound—tells Terminal to sound a beep whenever it receives a bell character (Ctrl-G). By default, Terminal will beep.

Carriage Return/Line Feed—tells Terminal how to interpret carriage returns. With the Inbound check box selected, Terminal will add a line feed to any inbound carriage return. With the Outbound check box selected, Terminal will add a line feed to any outbound carriage return. By default, Terminal adds no line feeds to carriage returns.

Cursor—sets the cursor to a block, an underline, a blinking block, or a blinking underline. The default setting is a blinking block.

Columns—specifies whether the screen should have 80 or 132 columns. The default is 80.

Terminal Font—determines the type of font and the point size used to display text. The default is usually the Fixed System font at 15 points.

Translations—sets the desired international character set for translation of textual data. Terminal uses as the default whatever character set you specified when you installed Windows; if you selected U.S., the default is None. If you have selected a language that has extended or accented characters, enable the IBM to ANSI option in Windows 3.1.

Show Scroll Bars—specifies whether or not scroll bars appear on the Terminal window. By default, they do appear.

Buffer Lines—sets the desired number of lines for the scroll buffer (the number of previously displayed lines that you can scroll back through). The default is 100.

Use Function, Arrow, and Ctrl Keys for Windows—in Windows 3.1, allows the use of these keys by Windows. If you disable the option, the keys will be used the way the remote terminal software indicates.

FUNCTION KEYS IN TERMINAL

Assigning Commands to Function Keys

Each of the first eight function keys (F1 through F8) can have up to 41 characters assigned to it. The function keys are given names, and can be displayed as buttons at the bottom of the screen. There are four sets, or levels, of function keys available, resulting in a total of 32 possible key assignments. You assign commands to function keys using the Function Keys dialog box.

Among other things, you can use function keys to automate your telecommunications sessions. For example, you could assign your CompuServe password and log-on name to a function key, and log on to that online service without all the tedious typing.

The left column is where you key in the function key's name, which will appear in the corresponding button at the bottom of the screen. The right column is where you key in the command that you wish the function key to execute. The Key Level option buttons allow you to switch to a new set of eight function key assignments. Select the Keys Visible check box if you wish the function key buttons to be displayed at the bottom of the screen once you close the Function Key dialog box. If Keys Visible is selected and you save the current settings to .TRM file, the function key buttons will be visible when you reload the file for your next session.

1. Pull down the Settings menu (Alt-S) and select Function Keys (K).

2. Type the desired name for the F1 function key button in the Key Name text box.

3. Click on the adjacent Command text box, or press Tab to move to it, then type the command you wish the function key to execute.

4. Repeat steps 2–3 for each function key, if desired.

5. Click on a Key Level option button, if desired, to make a new set of commands available, then repeat steps 2–3. (Press Alt-L to get to the Key Level option buttons, then select one using using the direction keys.)

6. Click on OK or press ↵.

Displaying the Function Keys

Function keys F1 through F8 can each have commands assigned to them. The keys are given names and can appear as buttons at the bottom of the Terminal screen. In its default state, Terminal does not display the function key buttons; however, changing this default is simple.

• Pull down the Settings (Alt-S) menu and select Show Function Keys (F). The bottom of the screen will display the function key buttons.

Invoking a Function Key

Invoking a function key means that you click on a function key button or press a function key to execute the command associated with that button or key.

- With the function key buttons visible (see "Displaying the Function Keys"), click on the function key button assigned to the command you wish to execute. Or, press and hold down the Ctrl and Alt keys, then press the function key that executes the command you want. (The F1 key is assigned to the left uppermost button. The F2 key is is assigned left lowermost button. The key assignments continue like that, odd-numbered buttons on the top row and even-numbered buttons on the bottom row, up to F8.) After the command executes, release the Ctrl and Alt keys.

THE SETTINGS FILE

Terminal allows you to save its settings in a file, which you can load for use the next time you call a given remote computer. These settings are explained under "Options," below. Terminal settings files have a .TRM extension.

1. Begin a new file by pulling down the File (Alt-F) menu and selecting New (N). A message box appears if you have changed any of the settings in the currently open file. Click Yes or press ↵ to save the changes, or No (Alt-N) to lose the changes. The current settings file is closed, and the settings are returned to the defaults. Go to step 5 to work with a new file. Open an existing file by pulling down the File (Alt-F) menu and selecting Open (O). The Open dialog box appears.

2. If necessary, select a different drive to locate the file you wish to open. Click on the arrow button or press Alt-V and then Alt-↓ to reveal the drop-down Drives list. Then click on the drive letter, or use the direction keys to highlight the drive letter and press Alt-↑.

3. If necessary, select a different directory to find the file. Double-click on the directory, or press Alt-D to move the cursor to the Directories list box, use the direction keys to highlight a directory, then press ↵.

4. Type the name of the file you wish to open in the File Name text box and press ↵. Or, double-click on the name of a file in the list box, or press Alt-N and then Tab to

     move the cursor to the list box, use the direction keys to highlight the file name, and press ↵.

5. Adjust all the settings to meet your needs (see "Options," below).

6. Pull down the File menu (Alt-F) and select Save (S). If the file was previously saved, it will be saved to the same file name. If the file is being saved for the first time, or if you selected Save As (A) from the File pull-down menu to save the file to a new name, the Save As dialog box will appear.

7. Type the file name in the File Name (Alt-N) text box. For information on saving the file to a new drive and or/directory, see "Saving a File Under a New Name."

8. Click OK or press ↵.

Options

Phone Number—lets you specify the telephone number of the host system you are calling.

Terminal Emulation—sets the type of terminal that Terminal should emulate for this session. See "Changing Terminal Emulation."

Terminal Preferences—allows you to change the specific characteristics of the current terminal emulation. See "Changing Terminal Settings."

Function Keys—enables you to assign character strings and some menu options to up to four sets of function keys. See "Assigning Commands to Function Keys."

Text Transfers—specifies the text transfer protocols.

Binary Transfers—specifies the binary transfer protocol to use for this session. See "Setting a Binary Transfer Protocol."

Communications—lets you change the communications parameters, such as baud rate, data bits, and parity, for the current session. See "Changing Communications Parameters."

Modem Commands—lets you change the commands Terminal transmits to the modem, such as the dialing prefix and the hang-up prefix and suffix.

Printer Echo—causes incoming text to be sent to the printer. If Local Echo is turned on (see "Changing Terminal Settings"), keystrokes are also sent to the printer.

Timer Mode—starts a timer running in the lower-right corner of the screen. This is useful for timing costly online sessions. The function keypad must be displayed (see "Displaying the Function Keys") for the timer to be displayed.

Show Function Keys—displays the function keys and their assignments in two rows at the bottom of the screen. Also displays a digital clock that can be used as a timer.

TEXT FILES

Capturing or Downloading a Text File

Terminal can either capture text to a file or download a text file from a remote terminal. When you capture text, every character sent by a remote terminal is sent to a text file. You should use the procedure below just before you capture or download a text file.

Before you transfer a text file, you must select how the flow of the text will be controlled. (See "Setting a Text Transfer Protocol".) Then you will be ready to receive a new text file, which may be added as a new file, appended to an existing file, or allowed to overwrite an existing file.

1. Pull down the Transfers menu (Alt-T) and select Receive Text File (R). The Receive Text File dialog box will appear.

2. Enable one or more of the options if desired. (See "Options," below.)

3. If necessary, select a different drive to store the text file. Click on the arrow button or press Alt-V and then Alt-↓ to reveal the drop-down Drives list. Then click on the drive letter, or use the direction keys to highlight the drive letter and press Alt-↑.

4. If necessary, select a different directory to store the text file. Double-click on the directory, or press Alt-D to move the cursor to the Directories list box, use the direction keys to highlight a directory, then press ↵.

5. Type the name of the new file, including the .TXT extension, in which you wish to store the received text in the File Name text box and press ↵. Or, double-click on the name of a file in the list box, or press Alt-N and then Tab to move the cursor to the list box, use the direction keys to highlight the file name, and press ↵. If you have selected a file name already in use, the Terminal-Error dialog box appears, asking if you wish to overwrite the file (unless you have selected to Append it—see "Options," below). Click Yes or press ↵. The text is downloaded to the specified file.

6. If you wish to stop the file transfer, click on the Stop button on the status line, or pull down the Transfers menu and select Stop (O). The file transfer can be temporarily stopped by clicking on the Pause button or pulling down the Transfers menu and selecting Pause (P). It can be restarted after pausing by clicking on the Resume button on the status line or by selecting Resume (R) on the Transfers pull-down menu.

Options   When capturing text files you have three options for how the incoming text should be saved and formatted:

Append File—instructs Terminal not to overwrite an existing file when an incoming text file has the same name. Terminal will append the new text to the text that already exists.

Save Controls—saves incoming control characters, which are characters that control screen formatting but are not themselves displayed on the screen. Though Terminal by default strips these characters away before saving a file to prevent your file from becoming muddled, there are times when saving control characters is necessary.

Table Format—saves incoming text in a tabular format. If characters are separated by two or more consecutive spaces, Terminal will place Tab characters between them.

Displaying a Text File

Before you send or after you have received a text file, you can view the contents of the file.

1. Pull down the Transfers menu (Alt-T) and select View Text File (V). The View Text File dialog box will appear.

2. Enable one of the options if desired (see "Options" in "Uploading a Text File").

3. If necessary, select a different drive to locate the text file you wish to see. Click on the arrow button or press Alt-V and then Alt-↓ to reveal the drop-down Drives list. Then click on the drive letter, or use the direction keys to highlight the drive letter and press Alt-↑.

4. If necessary, select a different directory to find the text file. Double-click on the directory, or press Alt-D to move the cursor to the Directories list box, use the direction keys to highlight a directory, then press ↵.

5. Type the name of the file you wish to see in the File Name text box and press ↵. Or, double-click on the name of a file in the list box, or press Alt-N and then Tab to move the cursor to the list box, use the direction keys to highlight the file name, and press ↵.

6. If you wish to stop the file contents from scrolling in the Terminal window, click on the Stop button on the status line, or pull down the Transfers menu and select Stop (O). The file scrolling can be temporarily stopped by clicking on the Pause button or pulling down the Transfers menu and selecting Pause (P). It can be restarted after pausing by clicking on the Resume button on the status line or by selecting Resume (R) on the Transfers pull-down menu. When the end of the file is reached or if you have stopped the display, you can use the vertical scroll bar, the PgUp or PgDn keys, or the direction keys to scroll through the file contents (up to the limit of the buffer).

Setting a Text Transfer Protocol

When you wish to transfer text files, Terminal allows you several options to control the flow of the transfer.

1. Pull down the Settings (Alt-S) menu and select Text Transfers (X). The Text Transfers dialog box appears.

2. Click on the option button or use the key sequence to select one of the three methods for controlling the flow of text (see "Options," below).

3. Enable the Word Wrap Outgoing Text at Column option and, if necessary, type a new value in the text box to specify the number of the column where the text will wrap.

4. Click OK or press ↵ to accept the selected options.

Options

Standard Flow Control (Alt-S)—(the default) uses the protocol specified in the Communications setting (see "Changing Communications Parameters").

Character at a Time (Alt-C)—sends text files one character at a time. You must then select Delay Between Characters (Alt-D), the default, to send each character with a specified interval before the next character in 1/10 second increments, or Wait for Character Echo (Alt-E), to allow the character to echo back for verification.

Line at a Time (Alt-L)—sends text file one line at a time. You must then select Delay Between Lines (Alt-D), the default, to send each line with a specified interval before the next line in 1/10 second increments, or Wait for Prompt String (Alt-P) to pause until a message is sent from the receiving computer.

Uploading a Text File

You can send a text file to a remote computer after you have selected a protocol for the text transfer (see "Setting a Text Transfer Protocol").

1. Pull down the Transfers (Alt-T) menu and select Send Text File (S). The Send Text File dialog box appears.

2. Enable one of the options if desired (see "Options," below).

3. If necessary, select a different drive to find the text file you wish to send. Click on the arrow button or press Alt-V and then Alt-↓ to reveal the drop-down Drives list. Then click on the drive letter, or use the direction keys to highlight the drive letter and press Alt-↑.

4. If necessary, select a different directory to find the text file. Double-click on the directory, or press Alt-D to move the cursor to the Directories list box, use the direction keys to highlight a directory, then press ↵.

5. Type the name of the file you wish to send in the File Name text box and press ↵. Or, double-click on the name of a file in the list box, or press Alt-N and then Tab to move the cursor to the list box, use the direction keys to highlight the file name, and press ↵. The selected text file is sent to the remote system.

6. If you wish to stop the file transfer, click on the Stop button on the status line, or pull down the Transfers menu and select Stop (O). The file transfer can be temporarily stopped by clicking on the Pause button or pulling down the Transfers menu and selecting Pause (P). It can be restarted after pausing by clicking on the Resume button on the status line or by selecting Resume (R) on the Transfers pull-down menu.

Options

Append LF (Alt-A)—attaches a line feed to every line sent.

Strip LF (Alt-S)—removes line feeds (the default) from the text sent.

Appendix

Object Linking and Embedding

In Windows 3.1, Microsoft introduced a new capability: object linking and embedding, also called OLE. With OLE, you can link or embed an object from a source (server) application's document to or in a target (client) application's document. The object can then be edited from inside the client document. An *object* can be a document, or it can be an icon—called a "package"—that represents the document or a part of it. For more information on objects and packages, see "Object Packager."

Four programs in Windows 3.1 support OLE. Write and Cardfile are both client applications—they receive objects in target documents. Paintbrush and Sound Recorder are both server applications—they provide objects from source documents. There are some applications (in programs other than Windows 3.1) that can be both client and server.

Linking defines a connection between two data files, one you are currently working on and another that is stored on disk and/or is being used by a different program. For example, you can use Paintbrush to open a graphic file you have created, and, using the Paste Link command, establish a link to the file on a Cardfile card and in a Write document. Whenever you edit the image in Cardfile, the image in the Write document and in Paintbrush reflects your changes.

Embedding places a complete copy of the object into the target document. If you embed a graphic image in a Windows Write document, for example, it is saved in the .WRI file that contains the document. Changes you make to the copy do not affect the object in the source document.

Linking and embedding are functionally very different. Which one you use depends on your individual needs. For example, you may wish to link a spreadsheet range to several files so that when information is updated in any of the files, all linked files are updated. Or, you may wish to embed a drawing in a document and edit that copy of the drawing; this leaves you free to later embed the original drawing (the source) in another document and edit it differently. The source drawing need not be changed when you edit your embedded drawings.

The following steps refer to the client and server applications in Windows 3.1.

EMBEDDING AN OBJECT

Objects can be embedded from either the client application or the server application.

Embedding an Object from the Client Application

1. With the client application open, position the insertion point where you wish the object to be embedded. Some client applications will always locate the object at the upper-left corner of the document or at the left margin.

2. If you are using Cardfile, pull down the Edit (Alt-E) menu and select Picture (E), even for a Sound Recorder file.

3. Pull down the Edit menu again and select Insert Object (N). The Insert New Object dialog box appears.

4. Double-click on the object type you wish to embed, or use the direction keys to highlight an object type in the list and press ↵. The application that will create the object opens.

5. Create a new object (drawing, package, or sound file). Or, in Paintbrush, pull down the Edit menu (Alt-E) and select Paste From (F) to open the document that includes the object you wish to use. In Object Packager, pull down the File (Alt-F) menu and select Import (I). In Sound Recorder, pull down the Edit menu and select Insert File (I). Double-click on the file you wish to open, or use the direction keys to highlight the file name and press ↵. Edit the object as necessary.

6. Pull down the File menu (Alt-F) and select Update (U) to insert the package in the document.

7. Pull down the File menu again and select Exit (X) in Object Packager and Sound Recorder, and Exit and Return to document name (X) in Paintbrush. In the message box that appears, click Yes or press ↵ to update the embedded object.

Embedding an Object from the Server Application

1. Open the application used to create the object.

2. Create the drawing or sound file, or open the file that contains the object.

3. If you are working with Paintbrush, select the drawing.

4. Pull down the Edit (Alt-E) menu and select Copy (C), or press Ctrl-C. The drawing or sound file is copied to the Clipboard.

5. Open the client application document.

6. In Cardfile, pull down the Edit (Alt-E) menu and select Picture (E) to embed a picture or a sound file.

7. Position the insertion point where you wish the object to be embedded. Some client applications will always locate the object at the upper-left corner of the document or at the left margin.

8. Pull down the client application's Edit (Alt-E) menu and select Paste (P), or press Ctrl-V. The object is embedded in the client application document.

Editing an Embedded Object

Objects created with a server application can be edited from within the document in which they are embedded.

1. If you are using Cardfile, select Picture from the Edit menu to edit your embedded document.

2. Double-click on the embedded object, or use the direction keys to select the object in Write, pull down the client application's Edit (Alt-E) menu, and select Edit Paintbrush Picture Object or Sound Object (O). From the Sound Object cascade menu, select Edit (E). The server application opens with the embedded file active in the document window.

3. Edit the server application file as needed.

4. Pull down the server application's File (Alt-F) menu and select Update (U).

5. Pull down the server application's File menu again and select Exit (X) or Exit and Return to document name (X). The server application closes and you are returned to the client application.

LINKING AN OBJECT

An object must be linked from a saved document. If the object is a Paintbrush drawing, a picture of the drawing appears in the target document. If the object is a sound file, the Sound Recorder icon appears in the target document. When you activate the icon, the sound file plays.

1. Open the server application.

2. Create a drawing or sound file and save it, or open an existing file.

3. If your object is a drawing, select it.

4. Pull down the server application's Edit (Alt-E) menu and select Copy (C), or press Ctrl-C.

5. Open the client application, and the file in which you wish to establish a link.

6. To establish a link in Cardfile, pull down the Edit (Alt-E) menu and select Picture (E).

7. Position the insertion point where you wish the object to be embedded. Some client applications will always locate the object at the upper-left corner of the document or at the left margin.

8. Pull down the client application's Edit (Alt-E) menu and select Paste Link (L). The drawing or sound file is inserted into the client application document.

9. Save the client application document.

Establishing More than One Link

You can link an object directly from the server application file (see "Linking Objects," above), as shown in Figure A.1. Or, you can establish a link to a client file by copying an existing link from a different client file, as shown in Figure A.2. Either method produces the same results—if one linked object is edited, all of the linked objects are changed to reflect the edits.

Copying an Existing Link

1. Open the client application document.

2. If the linked object is in Cardfile, pull down the Edit (Alt-E) menu and select Picture (E).

3. Click on the linked object you wish to edit, or use the direction keys to select the object.

4. Pull down the client application's Edit (Alt-E) menu and select Copy (C), or press Ctrl-C. The linked object is copied to the Clipboard.

5. Open the client application document into which you wish to place the copy of the linked object.

6. If the linked object is in Cardfile, pull down the Edit (Alt-E) menu and select Picture (E).

7. Position the insertion point where you wish the object to be embedded. Some client applications will always locate the object at the upper-left corner of the document or at the left margin.

8. Pull down the application's Edit (Alt-E) menu and select Paste (P), or press Ctrl-V. The linked object is inserted into the document.

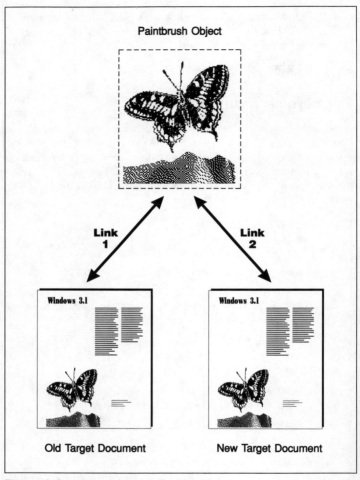

Figure A.1: Linking from the server file

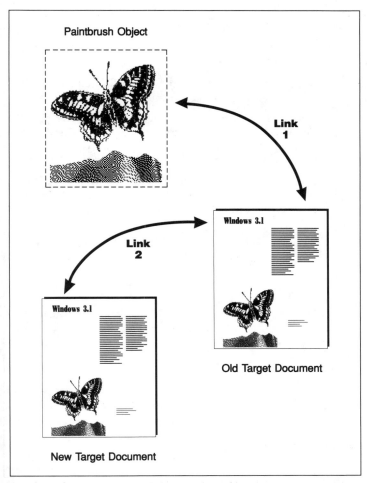

Figure A.2: Copying a link from a client file

Editing a Linked Object

When you edit a linked object, the changes are reflected in each file that is linked to the object.

1. If the linked object is in Cardfile, pull down the Edit (Alt-E) menu and select Picture (E).

2. Click on the linked object you wish to edit, or use the direction keys to select the object. (If the object is a Paintbrush drawing, double-click on it to open the file containing the drawing in Paintbrush.)

3. Pull down the client application's Edit (Alt-E) menu and select Edit Paintbrush Object or Sound Object (O). In the Sound Object cascading menu, select Edit (E).

4. Edit the object as necessary. If the object is a Paintbrush drawing, the changes are reflected in the drawing in the client application document.

5. Pull down the server application's File (Alt-F) menu and select Save (S) to save the changes to the file.

6. Pull down the server application's File menu again and select Exit (X). You are returned to the client application document.

Maintaining the Links

Once you have established a link, you can update the links, break or fix a link, or even delete a link that is no longer needed.

Breaking a Link

When you break a link, you break the connection between the server and the client applications in the document. The object can no longer be edited in the client application document, although the original file in the server application still exists.

1. Open the client application document that contains the linked object.

2. If the linked object is in Cardfile, pull down the Edit (Alt-E) menu and select Picture (E).

3. Click on the object, or use the direction keys to select it.

4. Pull down the client application's Edit (Alt-E) menu and select Links (K). The Links dialog box appears with the selected linked object highlighted in the list box.

5. Click on the Cancel Link (Alt-N) command button.

6. Click OK or press ⏎. The object is still in the client document, but is no longer linked to the server file.

Deleting a Link

When you delete a link, you remove the object and the link from the client document.

1. Open the client application document that contains the linked object.

2. If the linked object is in Cardfile, pull down the Edit (Alt-E) menu and select Picture (E).

3. Click on the object, or use the direction keys to select it.

4. Pull down the client application's Edit (Alt-E) menu and select Cut, or press Ctrl-X. The object and the link are deleted from the client document.

Repairing a Link

If the name of a server file containing a link is changed, all the links to that file will be broken—the client files are linked to a file that no longer exists. The links can be established to the new server file from within the linked client file(s). If you wish, you can also change an existing linked object to a different server (source) file.

1. Open the client application document that contains the broken link or the link you wish to change.

2. If the document is in Cardfile, pull down the Edit (Alt-E) menu and select Picture (E).

3. Click on the object, or use the direction keys to select it.

4. Pull down the client application's Edit (Alt-E) menu and select Links (K). The Links dialog box is displayed with the selected link highlighted.

5. Click the Change Link (Alt-H) command button. The Change Link dialog box is displayed.

6. Double-click on the new name of the renamed file in the File Names list box, or, press Tab to move the cursor to the list box, use the direction keys to highlight the new file name, and press ↵. The Change Link dialog box disappears, and the Links dialog box is displayed with the new file name selected.

7. Click OK or press ↵. If you selected a different source file, the new object appears in the client document.

Updating the Links

Linked objects are updated either automatically (the default) or manually. The object's appearance in the client document is affected if it is a drawing. If the object is an icon, its appearance in the document is not affected and the update setting does not matter.

To update automatically:

1. Open the client application document that contains the link.

2. If the document is in Cardfile, pull down the Edit (Alt-E) menu and select Picture (E).

3. Pull down the client application's Edit (Alt-E) menu and select Links (K). The Links dialog box is displayed.

4. In the Links (Alt-L) list box, click on the linked object(s) or use the direction keys to select the object(s) whose update option you wish to alter.

5. Click on the Automatic (Alt-T) option button to update the links as edits are made to the source. Or, click on the Manual (Alt-M) option button to allow the links to be updated at your discretion.

6. Click OK or press ↵ to change the update option for the selected link(s).

When you choose to update a link manually, the link (if it is an image rather than an icon) in the client document does not reflect any changes made to the source document until you decide to update it.

To update manually:

1. Open the client application document that contains the link.

2. If the document is in Cardfile, pull down the Edit (Alt-E) menu and select Picture (E).

3. Pull down the client application's Edit (Alt-E) menu and select Links (K). The Links dialog box is displayed.

4. In the Links (Alt-L) list box, click on the linked object(s) or use the direction keys to select the object(s) whose update option you wish to alter.

5. Click on the Update Now (Alt-U) command button.

6. Click OK or press ⏎ to update the link in the client document.

SELECTING A NEW FORMAT

Information copied from applications is sent and stored on the Clipboard in several different formats. This enables other applications to accept data from the Clipboard in the their own default formats. Use the Paste Special command to choose a different format than that selected by the target application before data is pasted or paste linked into it.

1. With the data you wish to embed or link copied to the Clipboard, open the client application document into which you wish to embed or link the data.

2. If the document is in Cardfile, pull down the Edit (Alt-E) menu and select Picture (E).

3. Position the insertion point where you wish the object to be linked or embedded. Some client applications will always locate the object at the upper-left corner of the document or at the left margin.

4. Pull down the client application's Edit (Alt-E) menu and select Paste Special (E). The Paste Special dialog box is displayed, with the default format selected for the data in Clipboard.

5. Click on a different format in the Data Type (Alt-D) list box, or use the direction keys to select a different format.

6.   Click Paste (Alt-P) to embed the new format, or Paste Link
(Alt-L) to link the new format in the client application.

Notes   The Paste Special command is not available in every Windows application. The file containing the data to be reformatted must
be saved in order for the Paste Special command to be available.

See Also   Cardfile, Microsoft Write, Object Packager, Paintbrush

Index

254 Index

Selections from The SYBEX Library

OPERATING SYSTEMS

The ABC's of DOS 4
Alan R. Miller

275pp. Ref. 583-2

This step-by-step introduction to using DOS 4 is written especially for beginners. Filled with simple examples, *The ABC's of DOS 4* covers the basics of hardware, software, disks, the system editor EDLIN, DOS commands, and more.

The ABC's of DOS 5
Alan Miller

267pp. Ref. 770-3

This straightforward guide will haven even first-time computer users working comfortably with DOS 5 in no time. Step-by-step lessons lead users from switching on the PC, through exploring the DOS Shell, working with directories and files, using essential commands, customizing the system, and trouble shooting. Includes a tear-out quick reference card and function key template.

ABC's of MS-DOS (Second Edition)
Alan R. Miller

233pp. Ref. 493-3

This handy guide to MS-DOS is all many PC users need to manage their computer files, organize floppy and hard disks, use EDLIN, and keep their computers organized. Additional information is given about utilities like Sidekick, and there is a DOS command and program summary. The second edition is fully updated for Version 3.3.

The ABC's of SCO UNIX
Tom Cuthbertson

263pp. Re. 715-0

A guide especially for beginners who want to get to work fast. Includes hands-on tutorials on logging in and out; creating and editing files; using electronic mail; organizing files into directories; printing; text formatting; and more.

The ABC's of Windows 3.0
Kris Jamsa

327pp. Ref. 760-6

A user-friendly introduction to the essentials of Windows 3.0. Presented in 64 short lessons. Beginners start with lesson one, while more advanced readers can skip ahead. Learn to use File Manager, the accessory programs, customization features, Program Manager, and more.

DESQview Instant Reference
Paul J. Perry

175pp. Ref. 809-2

This complete quick-reference command guide covers version 2.3 and DESQview 386, as well as QEMM (for managing expanded memory) and Manifest Memory Analyzer. Concise, alphabetized entries provide exact syntax, options, usage, and brief examples for every command. A handy source for on-the-job reminders and tips.

DOS 3.3 On-Line Advisor Version 1.1
SYBAR, Software Division of SYBEX, Inc.

Ref. 933-1

The answer to all your DOS problems.

The DOS On-Line Advisor is an on-screen reference that explains over 200 DOS error messages. 2300 other citations cover all you ever needed to know about DOS. The DOS On-Line Advisor pops up on top of your working program to give you quick, easy help when you need it, and disappears when you don't. Covers thru version 3.3. Software package comes with 3½" and 5¼" disks. **System Requirements:** IBM compatible with DOS 2.0 or higher, runs with Windows 3.0, uses 90K of RAM.

DOS Instant Reference
SYBEX Prompter Series
Greg Harvey
Kay Yarborough Nelson
220pp. Ref. 477-1

A complete fingertip reference for fast, easy on-line help:command summaries, syntax, usage and error messages. Organized by function—system commands, file commands, disk management, directories, batch files, I/O, networking, programming, and more. Through Version 3.3.

DOS 5: A to Z
Gary Masters
900pp; Ref. 805-X

A personal guru for every DOS 5 user! This comprehensive, "all you need to know" guide to DOS 5 provides detailed, A-to-Z coverage of DOS 5 commands, options, error messages, and dialog boxes—with syntax, usage, and plenty of examples and tips. It also includes hundreds of informative, in-depth articles on DOS 5 terminology and concepts.

DOS 5 Instant Reference
Robert M. Thomas
200pp. Ref. 804-1

The comprehensive quick guide to DOS—all its features, commands, options, and versions—now including DOS 5, with the new graphical interface. Concise, alphabetized command entries provide exact syntax, options, usage, brief examples, and applicable version numbers. Fully cross-referenced; ideal for quick review or on-the-job reference.

The DOS 5 User's Handbook
Gary Masters
Richard Allen King
400pp. Ref. 777-0

This is the DOS 5 book for users who are already familiar with an earlier version of DOS. Part I is a quick, friendly guide to new features; topics include the graphical interface, new and enhanced commands, and much more. Part II is a complete DOS 5 quick reference, with command summaries, in-depth explanations, and examples.

Essential OS/2
(Second Edition)
Judd Robbins
445pp. Ref. 609-X

Written by an OS/2 expert, this is the guide to the powerful new resources of the OS/2 operating system standard edition 1.1 with presentation manager. Robbins introduces the standard edition, and details multitasking under OS/2, and the range of commands for installing, starting up, configuring, and running applications. For Version 1.1 Standard Edition.

Essential PC-DOS
(Second Edition)
Myril Clement Shaw
Susan Soltis Shaw
332pp. Ref. 413-5

An authoritative guide to PC-DOS, including version 3.2. Designed to make experts out of beginners, it explores everything from disk management to batch file programming. Includes an 85-page command summary. Through Version 3.2.

Graphics Programming
Under Windows
Brian Myers
Chris Doner
646pp. Ref. 448-8

Straightforward discussion, abundant examples, and a concise reference guide to graphics commands make this book a must for Windows programmers. Topics range from how Windows works to programming for business, animation, CAD, and desktop publishing. For Version 2.

Inside DOS: A Programmer's Guide
Michael J. Young
490pp. Ref. 710-X

A collection of practical techniques (with source code listings) designed to help you take advantage of the rich resources intrinsic to MS-DOS machines. Designed for the experienced programmer with a basic understanding of C and 8086 assembly language, and DOS fundamentals.

Mastering DOS (Second Edition)
Judd Robbins
722pp. Ref. 555-7

"The most useful DOS book." This seven-part, in-depth tutorial addresses the needs of users at all levels. Topics range from running applications, to managing files and directories, configuring the system, batch file programming, and techniques for system developers. Through Version 4.

Mastering DOS 5
Judd Robbins
800pp. Ref.767-3

"The DOS reference to keep next to your computer," according to PC Week, this highly acclaimed text is now revised and expanded for DOS 5. Comprehensive tutorials cover everything from first steps for beginners, to advanced tools for systems developers—with emphasis on the new graphics interface. Includes tips, tricks, and a tear-out quick reference card and function key template.

UTILITIES

The Computer Virus Protection Handbook
Colin Haynes
192pp. Ref. 696-0

This book is the equivalent of an intensive emergency preparedness seminar on computer viruses. Readers learn what viruses are, how they are created, and how they infect systems. Step-by-step procedures help computer users to identify vulnerabilities, and to assess the consequences of a virus infection. Strategies on coping with viruses, as well as methods of data recovery, make this book well worth the investment.

Mastering the Norton Utilities 5
Peter Dyson
400pp, Ref. 725-8

This complete guide to installing and using the Norton Utilities 5 is a must for beginning and experienced users alike. It offers a clear, detailed description of each utility, with options, uses and examples—so users can quickly identify the programs they need and put Norton right to work. Includes valuable coverage of the newest Norton enhancements.

Mastering PC Tools Deluxe 6
For Versions 5.5 and 6.0
425pp, Ref. 700-2

An up-to-date guide to the lifesaving utilities in PC Tools Deluxe version 6.0 from installation, to high-speed back-ups, data recovery, file encryption, desktop applications, and more. Includes detailed background on DOS and hardware such as floppies, hard disks, modems and fax cards.

Norton Desktop for Windows Instant Reference
Sharon Crawford
Charlie Russell
200pp; Ref. 894-7

For anyone using Norton's version of the Windows desktop, here's a compact, fast-access guide to every feature of the package—from file management functions, to disaster prevention tools, configuration commands, batch language extensions, and more. Concise, quick-reference entries are alphabetized by topic, and include practical tips and examples.

Norton Utilities 5 Instant Reference
Michael Gross
162pp. Ref. 737-1

Organized alphabetically by program name, this pocket-sized reference offers complete information on each utility in the

Norton 5 package—including a descriptive summary, exact syntax, command line options, brief explanation, and examples. Gives proficient users a quick reminder, and helps with unfamiliar options.

Norton Utilities 6 Instant Reference
Michael Gross
175pp; Ref. 865-3
This pocket-size guide to Norton Utilities 6 provides fast answers when and where they're needed. Reference entries are organized alphabetically by program name, and provide a descriptive summary, exact syntax, command line options, brief explanations, and examples. For a quick reminder, or help with unfamiliar options.

PC Tools Deluxe 6 Instant Reference
Gordon McComb
194pp. Ref. 728-2
Keep this one handy for fast access to quick reminders and essential information on the latest PC Tools Utilities. Alphabetical entries cover all the Tools of Version 6—from data recovery to desktop applications—with concise summaries, syntax, options, brief explanations, and examples.

Understanding Norton Desktop for Windows
Peter Dyson
500pp; Ref. 888-2
This detailed, hands-on guide shows how to make the most of Norton's powerful Windows Desktop—to make Windows easier to use, customize and optimize the environment, take advantage of short-cuts, improve disk management, simplify disaster recovery, and more. Each program in the Norton Desktop gets thorough treatment, with plenty of practical examples.

Understanding the Norton Utilities 6 (Second Edition)
Peter Dyson
500pp; Ref. 855-6
Here is a detailed, practical sourcebook for PC users seeking to streamline their computing and extend the power of DOS with Norton 6. Features hands-on examples and up-to-date coverage of such topics as file management and security, hard disk maintenance, disaster recovery, and batch programming. Includes a complete command guide.

Understanding PC Tools 7
Peter Dyson
500pp; Ref. 850-5
Turn here for a complete guide to taking advantage of the new version of PC Tools for DOS 5 and Windows—with hands-on coverage of everything from installation to telecommunications. Special topics include networking; data security and encryption; virus detection; remote computing; and many new options for disk maintenance, disaster prevention, and data recovery.

Up & Running with Carbon Copy Plus
Marvin Bryan
124pp. Ref. 709-6
A speedy, thorough introduction to Carbon Copy Plus, for controlling remote computers from a PC. Coverage is in twenty time-coded "steps"—lessons that take 15 minutes to an hour to complete. Topics include program set-up, making and receiving calls, file transfer, security, terminal emulation, and using Scripts.

Up & Running with Norton Desktop for Windows
Michael Gross
David Clark
140pp; Ref. 885-8
Norton's new desktop utility package lets you customize Windows to your heart's content. Don't miss out! Learn to use this versatile program in just 20 basic lessons. Each lesson takes less than an hour to complete, and wastes no time on unnecessary detail.

Up & Running with Norton Utilities 5
Michael Gross
154pp. Ref. 819-0
Get a fast jump on Norton Utilties 5. In just 20 lessons, you can learn to retrieve erased files, password protect and

encrypt your data, make your system work faster, unformat accidentally formatted disks, find "lost" files on your hard disk, and reconstruct damaged files.

Up & Running with Norton Utilities 6
Michael Gross
140pp; Ref. 874-2

Come up to speed with Norton Utilities 6 in just 20 steps. This slim volume covers all of Norton's constituent programs (for both versions 5 and 6), provides command line syntax and options, and spells out the differences between versions 5 and 6 with special upgrade notes.

Up & Running with PC Tools Deluxe 6
Thomas Holste
180pp. Ref.678-2

Learn to use this software program in just 20 basic steps. Readers get a quick, inexpensive introduction to using the Tools for disaster recovery, disk and file management, and more.

Up & Running with XTreeGold 2
Robin Merrin
136pp. Ref. 820-3

Covers both XTreeGold 2 and XTreePro-Gold 1. In just 20 steps, each taking no more than 15 minutes to an hour, you can learn to customize your display, archive files, navigate the user interface, copy and back up your files, undelete accidentally erased files, and more.

NETWORKS

The ABC's of Local Area Networks
Michael Dortch
212pp. Ref. 664-2

This jargon-free introduction to LANs is for current and prospective users who see general information, comparative options, a look at the future, and tips for effective LANs use today. With comparisons of Token-Ring, PC Network, Novell, and others.

Mastering Novell NetWare
Cheryl C. Currid
Craig A. Gillett
500pp. Ref. 630-8

This book is a thorough guide for System Administrators to installing and operating a microcomputer network using Novell Netware. Mastering covers actually setting up a network from start to finish, design, administration, maintenance, and troubleshooting.

COMMUNICATIONS

Mastering Serial Communications
Peter W. Gofton
289pp. Ref. 180-2

The software side of communications, with details on the IBM PC's serial programming, the XMODEM and Kermit protocols, non-ASCII data transfer, interrupt-level programming, and more. Sample programs in C, assembly language and BASIC.

Mastering UNIX Serial Communications
Peter W. Gofton
307pp. Ref. 708-8

The complete guide to serial communications under UNIX. Part I introduces essential concepts and techniques, while Part II explores UNIX ports, drivers, and utilities, including MAIL, UUCP, and others. Part III is for C programmers, with six in-depth chapters on communications programming under UNIX.

Understanding PROCOMM PLUS 2.0 (Second Edition)
Bob Campbell
393pp; Ref. 861-0

This in-depth tutorial on communications with PROCOMM PLUS is now updated and expanded for version 2.0. It's still the best guide to PROCOMM PLUS, showing how to choose and install hardware; conncect with on-line services and other computers; send and receive files; create and use MetaKeys and scripts; and more.

WINDOWS SHORTCUT KEYS

IN WRITE

Key Sequence	Effect
F3	Find next occurrence
F4	Jump to specific page
F5	Make text normal
Ctrl-B	Make text boldfaced
Ctrl-I	Make text italic
Ctrl-U	Make text underlined
Ctrl-↵	Insert page break

IN PAINTBRUSH

Key Sequence	Effect
Ctrl-N	Zoom in
Ctrl-O	Zoom out
Ctrl-P	View picture
Ctrl-B	Make text boldfaced
Ctrl-I	Make text italic
Ctrl-U	Make text underlined
Ins	Left mouse button click
Del	Right mouse button click
F9-Ins	Left mouse button double-click
F9-Del	Right mouse button double-click